Court Reporting in Australia

T0300547

Court Reporting in Australia uses the experience of reporters and subeditors to present a practical view of reporting on the legal system. Peter Gregory avoids the rigid fashion in which media law matters are usually described and, while he covers such vital areas as defamation and contempt, he focuses on the experiences and lessons to be learned from court reporters on the job. He highlights the problems and common mistakes likely to land journalists and media organisations in trouble.

Court Reporting in Australia describes the different requirements for print and broadcast media. It features information and realistic advice from court reporters working for metropolitan media outlets as well as revealing how they perform their daily tasks. Practical and useful as well as theoretical, no one who reports on legal matters can afford to be without this book.

Peter Gregory is the Chief Court Reporter with *The Age* newspaper. He has been a journalist for 23 years, most of which has been spent covering courts.

Court Reporting in Australia

PETER GREGORY

CAMBRIDGE
UNIVERSITY PRESS

CAMBRIDGE UNIVERSITY PRESS
Cambridge, New York, Melbourne, Madrid, Cape Town,
Singapore, São Paulo, Delhi, Mexico City

Cambridge University Press
The Edinburgh Building, Cambridge CB2 8RU, UK

Published in the United States of America by Cambridge University Press, New York

www.cambridge.org
Information on this title: www.cambridge.org/9780521615112

First published 2005

A catalogue record for this publication is available from the British Library

National Library of Australia Cataloguing in Publication Data

Gregory, Peter John, 1959–.
Court reporting in Australia.
Bibliography.
ISBN 0 521 61511 9.
ISBN 9 78052161 5112.
ISBN-13 978-0-521-61511-2
ISBN-10 0-521-61511-9
1. Press law – Australia.   2. Newspaper court reporting – Australia.
3. Law reporting – Australia.   I. Title.
343.940998

ISBN 978-0-521-61511-2 Paperback

Contents

Figures and Tables

Figures

Tables

Acknowledgments

This book developed from training sessions held with young journalists. Fairfax training experts Colin McKinnon and Jacqui Cheng deserve recognition for their encouragement, as do the trainees, who kindly stayed awake during my talks.

Victorian Supreme court media officer Prue Innes has supported the project with information and contacts. She has been a great sounding board, and an enthusiastic supporter of open courts. Ms Innes, other court media representatives and administrators have been generous in answering my questions. They have answered promptly, sometimes at short notice.

The librarians at *The Age* are great researchers, and have been for many years. They are tremendous at turning speculative inquiries into concrete results. Court reporting colleagues have helped greatly by supplying examples and anecdotes, and taking part in the fictional exercise for one of our chapters. It was initially called 'Fun-filled Friday at the Courts', and promoted horror and creativity among the respondents.

Thanks are due to the media lawyers at Minter Ellison Lawyers, and the Communications Law Centre, for the information about defamation and contempt published in a number of media guides. They provided practical advice about difficult topics.

My first journalism lecturer, John Henningham, helped me in a number of ways. He supplied articles, gave advice about topics and chapter construction, and introduced me to Jill Henry, from Cambridge University Press. Ms Henry, as publisher, and her assistant, Karen Hildebrandt, kept me on track and reduced my doubts.

The greatest debt is owed to my wife, Julie, and daughter, Jess. They used patience, counselling and more patience to keep me on track. They also gave practical help in producing the manuscript, as did Claire Sasaki.

Finally, thanks to my parents, who bought books for me and encouraged me to study.

Introduction

Courts are a public mechanism for controlling behaviour and resolving disputes. They set standards of punishment and precedents for dealing with fights between governments, companies and individuals. But they are fascinating to the public for another reason – they are real. Criminal sanctions can cost real time in jail. Civil arguments can cost real money. Those who enter the public galleries can see real people at their best and worst under pressure.

Many excellent textbooks deal with the complexities of media law. They set out the statutes and cases relevant to journalists and their employers. A few provide hints for reporters – check the details of the case, don't read the newspaper in court, be courteous to court officials. This book does this too, but generally it aims to show how journalists report the courts day by day.

In the past, a few months working at the courts was an essential part of a journalist's cadetship. Dreams of exposing governments and writing features were put aside as the newest recruit clipped newspaper stories for the pressroom scrapbook or gathered adjournment dates for the diary. When they finally were allowed to report on a case, the cadet would be quizzed on the charges, the names of the lawyers and the magistrate (they would be lucky to report on the higher courts) and other basic details their mentors had written a thousand times. They would be taught discipline and respect for accuracy, and leave to start careers reporting on politics, sport or world affairs.

These were the stories the experienced court reporters at the big newspapers told. I started by accident, when the former courts roundsman left our afternoon paper and I failed to run away quickly enough. I had finished a media law subject in my university course, but a day or so with the departing reporter summed up the preparation. Our early deadlines meant it was hard to venture too far from the Brisbane Magistrates Court, where simple cases could be covered quickly (or was it quick cases covered simply?).

An experienced country journalist saved my bacon at the first murder trial I attended, in the Queensland town of Roma. A young local man was accused of two murders, and any lessons about the perils of contempt of court had obviously slipped my mind. At another afternoon paper in Adelaide, the education was more organised. The cadets were taken slowly through the courts. They had to earn the right to send stories, and graduated from minor cases and bail applications to reporting the State's major trials.

Journalism education has changed. Trainees take classes and workshops. They learn about their news organisation and are encouraged to think. At our newspaper, senior reporters give talks about their areas of expertise. Some of the trainees find their way to the courts, others work in a variety of journalistic disciplines.

This is an attempt to let young journalists and journalism students know what they will see if they are sent to the courthouse. News editors around the country no doubt will tell them how easy it is. You turn up, the stories are all there, all you do is wait for people to give them to you. After you spend some time at the round, it's easy to believe they are telling the truth. Lawyers and court staff get to know you. They tell you things. You find ways of obtaining documents and other information.

Then last year, the court hacks had to cover a case between two pressure groups adept at gaining publicity. Background material arrived at the office, complete with suggested interviewees and their telephone numbers. Photo opportunities could be organised, spokespeople could be found. When the hearing finished and the decision was made, the competing parties were happy to supply more quotes, and declare themselves the winner (or at least, the non-loser). One fellow offered to supply the background material again. This was money for jam.

The daily reality of covering courts is that the judges and lawyers believe with some justification that they could do their job successfully and probably with less difficulty if media interests were not present. They do not need journalists to help them sell products or get them re-elected. They have been professionally trained. If anything, many believe court reports distort their messages about crime and punishment to the community. Some of them make reporters work for basic pieces of information that would help accuracy. They suppress information swiftly, and use complex language which hides the real intent of their orders.

Court veterans can remember sitting for hours as judicial officers read every word of a significant ruling before announcing the decision. Somehow, I missed a six-hour effort by one judge, but watched the clock as a shorter effort slowly put pressure on an early Friday deadline. The story made the front page, which was held as late as possible so we could accurately interpret the judgment. Did we? It's hard to know. There were no complaints on the following Monday. New stories were on the way by then, so we looked forward to them.

Technology has changed the position. Judges are accustomed to electronic communication. It is commonplace, not revolutionary, to make multiple copies of important decisions, and distribute them around the country. The employment of court media officers has helped as well. They have a job to promote and protect their court, but their daily role lies in the 'nuts and bolts' work of advising on information access, checking suppression orders and obtaining written decisions. Criticism of sexist comments and perceived light sentences has angered judges, but their courts are adapting by making knowledge easier to get. Critics cannot trade on ignorance if everyone can know what the court said.

Reporters are changing as well. They are better educated and more likely to challenge the traditional notion of objectivity that underpins court reporting. They are quick to move from the round if they are denied opportunity. But they learn quickly, and seem to show less fear of disturbing legal convention.

Despite this, some truths remain. The need for accuracy, the desire to listen and the ability to translate legalese into ordinary language are still prized skills. Today, the job in our pressroom was to reduce a 215-page judgment into an eleven-paragraph story. It is impossible to retain the detail and breadth of argument in such a reduction. The aim was to find the essence of the case and convey it while recording the result.

In one sense, this text has a similar ambition. It seeks to place readers in the reporter's shoes, just as the court story should place its audience in the courtroom. It will discuss story writing, obtaining information, and the relationships entered with colleagues and court workers. A 'reality reporting' exercise on a busy Friday (Chapter 9) shows how one group of working journalists approaches an exhausting work agenda. Other chapters describe the perspectives of radio and television reporters, subeditors and photographers.

One chapter examines the practicalities of obtaining information from the court system. Administrators and media officers set out the access available to media workers and the cost of searching files. With the help of other guides, chapters on contempt, suppression orders and defamation discuss legal hurdles which reporters confront every day.

Chapter 1

The Court System: An Overview

Courts are society's mechanism for enforcing its laws. Their purpose is to protect individuals and their property, to let our economic and parliamentary frameworks operate and protect the community as a whole. The Australian legal system, based on British law, is commonly called a hierarchical one. Minor cases, like small thefts and assault, or less serious breaches of traffic rules, are heard at one end of the system, usually called Magistrates or Local courts. At the other end, the High Court hears constitutional arguments and is the final appeal court for Australian cases. Parliaments make laws; so do judges by the decisions they make in court. Court-made law is otherwise known as common law. Laws have been developed to handle perceived breaches of rules and a variety of other disputes. Criminal courts hear evidence, make decisions and impose sanctions for offences ranging from parking fines to murder and treason. Civil hearings deal with arguments over contracts and non-criminal wrongs by one party resulting in loss or harm to another. Claims for compensation for personal injury caused by negligence or damage to reputation from defamation fall into this category. Family break-ups and the surrounding issues are another. A range of behaviour involving children is administered by a separate court, although the more serious offences can be heard in the adult system. Commonwealth laws, deaths, financial and broadcasting cases and migration debates are all covered within the court hierarchy. Tribunals, designed to be less formal and less expensive than the courts, have been developed to sort out arguments in a more efficient way. Appeals can be made to the court system, but resolution is encouraged. In a similar way, mediation between parties, with a trained lawyer or quasi-legal officer facilitating discussion,

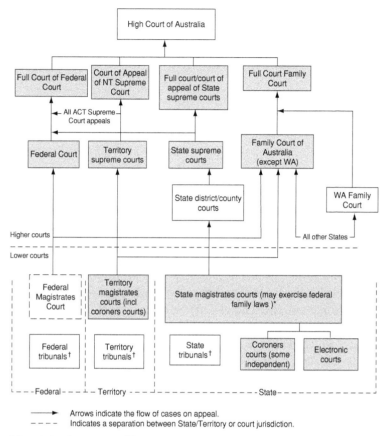

Arrows indicate the flow of cases on appeal.
Indicates a separation between State/Territory or court jurisdiction.

* Appeals from lower courts in NSW go directly to the Court of Appeal in the NSW Supreme Court.
† Appeals from Federal, State and Territory tribunals may go to any higher court in their jurisdiction.

Figure 1.1   The court hierarchy (Source: Australian Bureau of Statistics, published in *Year Book Australia* 2002)

is another method of seeking an end to a dispute without the cost and formality of going to court.

Mediation is a method that tries to avoid the most confrontational aspects of the usual adversarial approach of the courts. Unlike some systems, in which a tribunal of judges supervise what is said to be a search for the truth, parties in our structure present conflicting arguments before judicial officers or judges and juries. In a criminal trial, an accused is presumed innocent, and the prosecuting authorities must prove their case at the highest legal standard, beyond reasonable doubt, to gain a conviction. An accused person is not required to give evidence. The judge in a jury trial decides on the law, and which evidence is admissible or able to be presented before the jury. Jurors are told they are judges of the facts – they determine the facts of the case based on the evidence before them. They are not allowed to be investigators, and trials have been aborted, or cancelled, to be started again before a new jury, because jurors have used the internet or conducted their own inquiries outside the trial. Prosecutors at a criminal trial sit closest to the jury at the bar table. They have a duty to present all relevant evidence, and represent the community by bringing the charge or charges against an accused person. In the lower courts, police prosecutors with specific training present the prosecution case. Lawyers known as barristers address the court in the higher jurisdictions. Senior barristers, known as Queen's Counsel, or Senior Counsel, may have another barrister (described as junior counsel) to help them. Their instructing solicitor, who prepares the case, sits opposite them at the bar table. Defence counsel represent their clients. They may call evidence, but are not obliged to do so. Like prosecutors, they can test evidence through cross-examination. In a practical sense, defence counsel can be more likely to ask for evidence or publication of material to be excluded in the interests of the accused.

Civil cases generally are decided on the balance of probabilities. One colloquial definition was whether a proposition was more likely than not to be correct. Juries can sit in civil cases in some jurisdictions. For example, Victorian courts have six-member juries in personal injury and defamation cases, but barristers can argue to have the matter heard by judge alone. In civil cases, a plaintiff, who brings the action, will ask for an order or declaration to be made, and often for monetary compensation to make up for the wrong alleged to have been done. A respondent can admit or deny liability for the claimed wrong. If liability was admitted in a personal injury case, the parties could then argue about the amount of compensation to be paid.

Journalists receive a qualified privilege to report fairly and accurately on court proceedings. The privilege means they are not liable to be sued for repeating the frequently defamatory remarks made in the courtroom as disputes are fought out. They are given the privilege through the tradition in British justice of open courts.

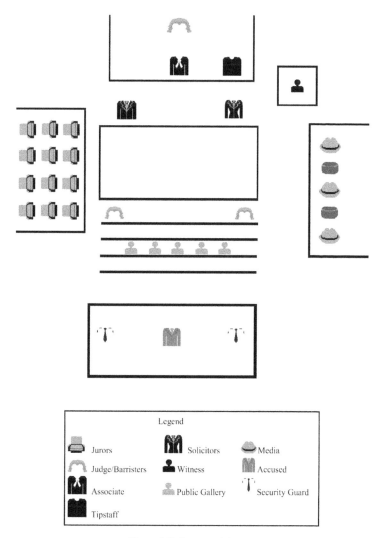

Figure 1.2 Court participants

Some theorists say the open court principle derived from an Anglo-Saxon practice that required all members of a manor, including the lord and serfs, to attend and pass judgment on perceived wrongs. There are competing theories about the development of open courts from supposedly secretive inquisitorial bodies like the Star Chamber. One theory suggests open hearings represented a backlash against such private and punitive inquiries. The other theory is that having severe punishment imposed in an open proceeding had a greater deterrent effect. Media law researchers Robertson and Nicol (1990) say the open hearing rule became established almost by accident, because courts in the Middle Ages were badly conducted public meetings in which neighbours gathered to pass judgment on their district's notorious felons. The United States Supreme Court, in a 1979 judgment on public trial rights, said the concept was firmly established by the 17th century, and there was little record of secret hearings, criminal or civil.

The legal writer Blackstone said in 1765 that the liberty of the press was essential to the nature of a free state, but those who published improper, mischievous or illegal material had to take the consequences of their actions. The view is a starting point to understanding court reporting today. Journalists do not have an absolute right to freedom of speech in Australia. Laws regulate and balance public discussion and the transfer of information. The issue in courts is often described as a balancing exercise between the rights of an accused to a free trial and the ability to disseminate information from an open court. In 1999, Lord Irvine of Lairg, the British Lord Chancellor, said the media had a unique and constitutionally acknowledged role to ensure that justice was seen to be done. Journalists received practical access to information from the legal system that exceeded the rights generally given to the public. He quoted British judges who observed that any curtailment of media rights was a similar brake on public access to the administration of justice, and that a truly democratic society could not tolerate the void left if casual observers, not a daily media commentary, were the basis for information from courts. Lord Irvine said the primary and fundamental purpose of every court was the delivery of justice according to law. But an accompanying principle was that justice must be delivered openly.

Despite the lack of a constitutional free speech guarantee, these principles show that media organisations have a role in communicating court proceedings. Their employees are rewarded with operational privileges as they cover the courts each day. They have seats set aside in the courtroom to let them hear submissions. Courts regularly make rooms available for journalists, on either a permanent or ad hoc basis, so they can work from the judicial premises. Copies of sentencing remarks, judgments, court exhibits and transcripts can be set aside so that the task of sending information to the public is made easier. Rules designed to protect fair trials are restrictive, but journalists or their legal representatives have the opportunity to ask that orders are varied or rescinded. Court reporters are effectively part of the legal system. They stand to one side observing and describing the daily legal struggle. But they are also reminded about their responsibilities to report accurately and in a way that lets the legal process continue unhindered.

At a 1999 conference on courts and the media, Australian legal writer David Solomon said the media's duty was to report what happened in the courts, and provide intelligent and critical analysis of them. Justice Susan Kiefel, from the Federal Court, referred at the same conference to a professor's earlier description of judges' perceptions of the media. The perception included that the media was superficial, biased, inadequate, sensational, inaccurate, unfair, misleading, irresponsible and damaging to the public interest. Quoted in *Medialine* magazine from an earlier speech (1998–99), Justice Bernard Teague from the Victorian Supreme Court nominated judges' concerns about the media, including misrepresentation, ill-informed criticism, taking remarks out of context and using other agendas to colour court reports. He said judges had high expectations that court reports should be accurate. One judge was furious after being attacked for leniency in sentencing when the media report said the maximum term imposed in a criminal case was five years, not the fifteen years actually ordered. Justice Teague pointed to communication and improved access as ways to improve accuracy.

Others point to the commercial nature of media outlets as a barrier to reasonable court coverage. Australia has prominent public broadcasters, but most media outlets are run by commercial companies whose objectives are to make money. Audiences are delivered to advertisers through the selection of information thought to appeal to the desired part of the market. Media companies boast of attracting high-income 'AB' customers, or appealing to a youth market, or leading the ratings determined by surveys. From the hundreds of court hearings on a given day, reporters might agree on the 'big' stories but also be aware of the sorts of cases their employer would prefer. Some publications would report on unionists in court only if they were likely to be sent to jail. Others would concentrate on cases involving parties from the demographic group they want to serve. Most have taken advantage of the greater interest in victims' rights to question penalties and find outrage at leniency.

Associate law professor Elizabeth Handsley, speaking at a forum in 2004 concerned with the reform of contempt of court laws, said media public spiritedness and sense of duty was a good thing, but it had to coexist – sometimes uncomfortably – with the drive for ratings and readership. Press freedom might not be exercised in the public good unless that amounted to giving the public what it wanted and satisfied its curiosity. She argued that press freedom should be justified by giving people what they needed or what was in the public interest. Lord Irvine, in a 1999 lecture about media rights and responsibilities, said the media acted for the public, but was not the public. All forms of media reporting involved filters which selected information to publish. He was concerned that economic and market pressures increasingly shaped the filtering process. News was a commodity, he said, with a cash value attached.

Many journalists see court reporting as among the least commercial of the journalistic rounds at a news company. Advertisers shy away from giving the free products and junkets that appear to inhabit other areas of the craft. Unlike politicians, many lawyers and judges shun publicity. They do not need to attract votes. They question why journalists should be able to hold up proceedings with legal applications when they are merely businesses engaged in making money. Some argue that court proceedings should not be reported at all until the whole appeal process has finished, so that inflammatory stories cannot have any chance of influencing juries. It is true that big cases attract blanket coverage, probably more than in the recent past as television finds more ways of marrying pictures with news from the courts. But the daily reality outside the high-profile murders, compensation claims and defamation actions is a quest to find 'filler' stories for the back pages of newspapers or the end of bulletins. Court reporting was traditionally seen as a way of showing young journalists the need for accuracy and impressing on them the basics of journalism. Working at the courts was not an end in itself but a stepping stone to greater opportunity. The reporters who stayed were seen as experts in not writing stories, glancing at shadows as they saw potential effects on trials in the mildest of articles.

Why stay then? Courts contain conflict and drama, two staples of newsgathering. They appeal to the voyeur in ordinary citizens; they show the way laws and decisions by business and government impact on the community through the examples of a few. The cases test the good taste of journalists, some of whom will ask any question to have a victim or family member cry on camera. But the public is interested, even if it amounts to mere curiosity. Michael Connor, in his book about Australia's first newspaper, describes the fascination of readers with the big murder case of 1803. The finding of a murdered constable was described in fairly graphic detail in the report. Four men were tried, three of them acquitted. A faulty rope saved the convicted man from hanging and he was granted a reprieve. Connor (2004) says readers followed the twists and turns of the case in dramatic weekly episodes published in the *Sydney Gazette*. The public is interested in a good story. Readers react to human struggle, sadness, anger. It is easy to see how those values differ from those of the judiciary, who declare their interest is a just result from a trial based on objectivity, not emotion. Nevertheless, it seems that restricting court coverage to 'public interest' cases would be counterproductive. Who would police them? How would they decide? Would anyone read them? As a journalist, I am going to be biased in favour of disclosure and a lack of restrictions for all court reporting. It might be that some laws which prevent or delay publication are justified, but some legal minds need little encouragement to expand them exponentially.

Many courts have seen information as the answer. Provide more, and journalists might be more likely to get it right. It puts more pressure on reporters to avoid 'beat-ups' if they know everyone will have access to the material on which they base their stories. In some jurisdictions, media websites include a link to the full transcript of judgments or published sentencing remarks. The link is shown alongside the court report. Practical work is required to have the link in place, but I am amazed that courts have not tried this more often. Readers can be very critical of media outlets and can embarrass media outlets into changing policy where professionals who complain have little effect. Perhaps more communication, not less, is the key to ensuring the media behaves itself.

Chapter 2

Gaining Information

Every five weeks or so, the High Court is on the move. Two or three judges will sit in a State capital to hold a number of short hearings. They are deciding whether to grant permission for appeals to be heard at the court, the pinnacle of Australia's legal hierarchy. Leading barristers operating in State and federal courts mix with litigants in person (members of the public presenting their cases without a legal advocate) as they try to convince the court to hear their full appeal. Not many succeed. The High Court heard 389 applications for special leave to appeal in 1999–2000, but only sixty-six were accepted for further consideration. In those cases, a larger panel of judges hears the appeal arguments at a later date, makes a ruling, and later publishes a decision which will affect future legal proceedings throughout the country.

The court sees its role as upholding the Constitution, maintaining the rule of law and acting as Australia's final court of appeal in civil and criminal matters. The judges will grant special leave where they see a legal issue as important enough to decide, or where there has been a significant irregularity in the way in which a lower court has dealt with a case. The special leave hearings usually attract a crowd. Law students, interested members of the public, lawyers and lobbyists often pack the courtrooms set aside for the hearings. They are 'limited submission' affairs, twenty minutes of argument per side with a warning light showing after eighteen. Observers have the chance to see some of the best legal minds operating under severe pressure of time. The entertainment value was increased by the placing of the warning lights at the front of the judicial bench. When the yellow light flashed, the two-minute countdown for final submissions began. Unfortunately, the system has been modified by the subsequent placement of the lights on the barrister's lectern. Now spectators need a reasonable vantage point to check when advocates must speed up arguments, or abandon their worst ones, as they struggle to meet the deadline. The judges can grant more time, or choose not to hear one of the parties before deciding whether to grant special leave. The reward for the successful applicant is a longer hearing at a later date on questions of law. The penalty for a failed bid is the realisation that there are no more appeals in the legal system.

High Court hearings can sound incomprehensible for those without advance knowledge of a case. The barristers (and judges) will argue about the application of laws, and rarely mention interesting circumstances of a case. Reporters can help themselves by keeping in touch with local matters listed for appeal. Crime, migration, financial and constitutional fights find their way to special leave day. Reporters can search the files, but that process should not be left until the last minute. The judges prefer to read the paperwork in advance to prepare themselves; reporters should do likewise. Files are held in a limited number of registries (see below), so it may take time to get access to the documents. Migration matters involving protection visa applications require the removal of the applicants' identity. This also takes time and reinforces my advice to get in early with searches. The High Court has short summaries of special leave applications which can be obtained before the hearings.

Lawyers and parties fighting matters of principle can also be useful to the reporter. Make it clear you are interested in documents and want to know when they are due to appear. Arming yourself with information and arranging photographs and potential interviews at the court can make it easier to inform the public. It makes the story easy to sell to a news editor. If the reporter cannot explain what the case is about to others at the office, he or she is going to have a hard time getting the story published.

Advance knowledge of the case and the ability to illustrate it with material from outside court helps promote even a complicated case. The Yorta Yorta people, an Aboriginal community living near the New South Wales–Victoria border, kept media interest in their native title claim by being available outside court and delivering a simple message in a complicated battle. The fight ended unsuccessfully in the High Court, but talks continued later with government interests. Similarly, family members of an elderly widow killed at her home kept the case alive in the media by flying to Canberra and making themselves the pictorial focus of the story. Lobbying families can face disappointment at the High Court. They might feel rightly aggrieved that their pain continues as the convicted perpetrator of a crime explores all his or her appeal rights. But the rights act as a safeguard against injustice. Reporters are entitled to question the rules and decisions made in court, but media audiences are equally entitled to know the issues. It is very easy to campaign on behalf of the 'good guys' – slam the killers, attack their appeals and promote anger at them and sympathy for the victims. It is harder to remind audiences that the legal system is supposed to apply equally for everyone, even convicted criminals apparently hated by the public. It might take more time, space and effort, but it is fairer and more informative to report appeal grounds as fully as possible. In other cases, journalists are accused of maintaining the status quo by maintaining a so-called even-handed approach when one side should receive a pasting for their moral position. Aside from questions of privilege (see Chapters 3 and 10), I think the best service journalists can do for their readers in such cases is to report openly and give as much information as possible. News organisations can and should campaign. They should also tell their audiences when they are campaigning, when they are commenting and when they are producing a 'straight' report. The worst stories, in my view, are those which pretend to be balanced but quietly take a position. They choose the facts that suit their argument and eliminate or minimise those that favour the opposition. A report from court can be one-sided, but the public should know the reporter is taking that side. No doubt it is true, as many commentators argue, that journalists writing 'objective' reports will draw on their prejudices and interests when selecting the information to be published. They will also assess the interests of their publishers, so some topics will be ignored because they cannot be sold to the perceived interests of the media outlet's audience.

But I believe audiences are not as stupid as some think. They realise that most media companies are commercial organisations which choose entertaining or dramatic cases to report. They understand that news reports are supposed to be even-handed. If community response through surveys and phone calls to individual journalists are to be believed, they are suspicious of media motives. In my view, the journalist's first aim should be to inform the public. Eliminate your prejudice as best you can and try to provide context and balance. Readers are and should be wary about attempts to tell them how to think. Sometimes they have tremendous conspiracy theories about the perceived reasons for media organisations publishing one story over another, or choosing one part of a story over another. Showing fairness to the worst convicted criminal hopefully indicates you are open to the prospect of writing the truth.

Australian media organisations have been criticised for their coverage of High Court hearings. Few, if any, have permanent reporters. Instead, journalists from political bureaus in Canberra inherit the High Court as part of their job. State and Territory-based reporters follow specific cases as they progress through the legal system. This approach tends to mean that major stories such as native title claims or criminal cases are covered, but that the court's regular work is under-reported. The words 'landmark' and 'test case' are essential for court reporters trying to persuade their bosses they should be allowed to travel interstate for full hearings. Some years ago, a journalist from a competing paper and I managed such a trip to Queensland, each using the excuse that the opposition was going and our organisation did not want to be left out. Fortunately, each had made a trip to the High Court registry and had searched the court file. We had a reasonable knowledge about the case, and found that the stories we wrote were about a day ahead of those prepared by the local journalists. My competitor would have been happy about having the advantage, except that none of his stories were published. We were there for about two days, and had he packed his crystal ball he might have spent the time at the beach.

Appeals from the Federal Court and State Supreme courts provide the bulk of cases presented for debate before the High Court bench. The Federal Court deals with disputes under Commonwealth laws, such as those concerning copyright, trade practices, intellectual property, elections and discrimination. These are not necessarily as dry as they sound. One intellectual property dispute involved the founding members of the Little River Band (some younger reporters desperately tried to remember original song titles). An electoral case featured a protest by an independent candidate who wanted to retain his advantage as the first name on the ballot paper, despite there being a mishap with the machine which determined the order of names selected.

But the Federal Court case that provided the most reader feedback to my telephone extension was a discrimination application brought by a disabled rights activist. In short, she claimed to have suffered prejudice at a suburban swingers' party, a gathering at which guests attended (mostly) as couples and engaged in friendly contact with other consenting adults. The party host denied the claim that the activist suffered discrimination and ultimately won the case. It seemed everyone I met remembered the hearing and the media reports from it. Even those who did not read bylines had little trouble recalling the subject matter. 'You wrote that story? What was it like in the court?' Years of writing worthy pieces from applications that challenged laws or protested in big national issues had left the court reporters unused to the attention.

Similarly, an application by a pregnant national league netball player to overturn restrictions placed by her sport's ruling body gathered considerable short-term publicity. It is a lesson to court reporters to think laterally – don't assume that cases in the federal jurisdiction will be worthy but not very exciting or readable. A hearing of the Defence Forces Tribunal, administered by a Federal Court judge, featured the difficulties encountered by a serviceman who found that his home-made adult video had been seized unintentionally when authorities were making checks at his home. Many of the federal cases are important, and should be reported, but there is room for less significant matters.

State appeal courts rule on commercial, civil and criminal cases, but crime and punishment command the most media attention. Judges, sometimes correctly, complain that they can increase sentences in numerous appeals concerning convicted murderers and rapists, but the only decisions reported are those in which the sentences are reduced. As they would see it, conflict sells newspapers. It is a lot easier to find critics and commentators when judges make rulings that seemingly let criminals avoid punishment. Victims are quoted, columnists slam 'out of touch' judges, lobbyists call for tougher penalties, momentum builds as new angles for the story are found over several days. Compare that with the single day's run in the newspaper earned by reporting an increased sentence, or the difficulties in selling a prisoner's rights story that originates in the appeal court.

It takes more effort to report appeal hearings, which can continue for days, than it does to wait for a published judgment weeks later. Appeal hearings tend to feature argument about technicalities and legal mistakes rather than the facts of a case. Reporters have no guarantee that they will receive a copy of appeal grounds, or the response by the opposing party. Some barristers explain their arguments in simple terms, so an observer walking into court without prior knowledge of the case would have a fair chance of understanding what was happening. Others are happy to refer to 'paragraph three of our submissions, your Honours', then spend half an hour describing relevant precedents. Careful listening helps, especially during boring argument. It means the reporter has specific questions to ask at the next break. It must be very frustrating for barristers, who are paid advocates, to be asked after 150 minutes on their feet what the case was about. There is no disgrace in asking a basic question, but asking a thoughtful question based on the material that anyone could have heard by sitting in court can yield more helpful information.

The Supreme Court hears the most important civil cases in the State, criminal prosecutions for offences such as murder and treason, and usually deals with injunction applications for urgent or important issues. Defamation actions and major personal injury cases are frequently heard in the Supreme Court. It sounds disrespectful to say so, but murder trials are the 'bread and butter' of the court reporter's job.

It is true that the media report regularly and selectively on murder trials. The cases can contain the most drama; they have the most severe consequences for the victim and often the highest penalties for convicted offenders. According to the Australian Bureau of Statistics, the number of murders in the country fell by 5 per cent in 2003, but 938 were recorded across the States and Territories. That figure does not include separate results for manslaughter, driving causing death, and attempted murder. Many of those charged plead guilty (1249 in the Victorian Supreme and County courts in

2001–02, compared with 377 trials), and in many courts a number of trials are run at the same time. In those circumstances, journalists must choose, and they will opt for cases they believe their organisations will publish.

Organised crime killings, murders of strangers by dangerous offenders, emotional cases such as so-called mercy killings are almost guaranteed to attract interest. Domestic killings are said to make up about half the reported murders, and are probably under-reported at trials. But cases which might be seen as representative of a wider social problem, or as having been committed in unusual circumstances, will be covered. Provocation defences brought by men who killed their wives, women who kill after suffering years of domestic violence, and, in one case, a 20-year family feud which resulted in murder are examples of issues represented by criminal trials. Major personal injury and defamation cases, commercial fights between large companies and injunction bids are other cases which fall within the Supreme Court boundaries.

The larger States have intermediate courts, called the District and County courts, which deal with a variety of indictable offences (those sent for trial from lower courts). They include armed robbery, sex offences, drug-related crimes and serious assaults. The official statistics show that 158 629 assaults and 19 719 robberies were recorded across Australia in 2003. Many of those cases might be dealt with in the lower courts, but it indicates the potential court business generated by criminal activity.

The intermediate courts can be the sources of stories sparked by media interest in specific topics. Courts have increased penalties for driving causing death, and media outlets have fed on the emotion and terrible consequences of killings related to speed, alcohol and drugs. The investigations and prosecutions of child pornography collectors and child sex offenders have meant that reporters will cover the stories knowing they will be run. Anecdotally, media outlets have chosen not to publish child sex stories regularly because they seemed to be exploitative and were seen to repel audiences. Trends change. In late 2004, the number of adults in responsible jobs found to be holding pornographic images of children gave a new reason for publicising cases which otherwise might not have been given prominence.

The Magistrates or Local courts provide the starting points for most legal cases in the Australian system. Magistrates hear cases ranging from murder to jaywalking. They deal with minor offences or complaints in summary hearings and refer more important matters to higher courts through preliminary proceedings known as committals. Some of those cases are obvious media targets, but the more trivial can also be newsworthy. Musicians or sportspeople caught behaving badly, neighbourhood disputes gone wrong, stupid decisions made while offenders were drunk – all can be entertaining.

Early one January during the late 1980s, a young New Year's Eve reveller pleaded guilty to punching a police horse. The public gallery erupted in laughter, and even the barristers cracked a smile. One spectator ran from the court, trying to suppress his mirth. The offender looked serious and the magistrate criticised the hilarity, pointing out the dangers of the assault. But memories of a similar scene in the comedy film *Blazing Saddles*, regularly shown on television, were too fresh. The absurdity of what must have seemed like a good idea at the time to the unfortunate assailant meant that local newspapers were happy to carry the story. Human frailties, especially very silly ones, make news just as readily as important events. The key is to know when to stop. When you are trying too hard to find puns that suit a supposedly quirky story pursued as entertainment value, it's time to leave the case alone.

Coronial inquests can be the saddest of hearings to cover. They investigate suspicious or unusual deaths, ranging from tragedies and apparent domestic violence involving children to accidents on jet boats or at train crossings. Coroners frequently make safety recommendations in an effort to prevent future deaths in specific circumstances.

The Family and Children's courts restrict publication of their proceedings, largely to protect children. The court websites spell out the laws which restrict publication and the exceptions. Names and photographs can be published to help authorities find a missing child. The Family Court has a list of missing children or their parents whose identities can be published. Judicial officers must make orders allowing the release of photographs and information. If in any doubt about using information from these courts, make

sure you check. Quite apart from the public interest in protect-
ing children, identifying parties and witnesses to Family Court
proceedings, for example, attracts a maximum punishment of a
year in jail.

State and federal tribunals process complaints on topics as
diverse as planning, discrimination, human rights issues and freedom of information. The hearings are less formal than ordinary
court proceedings, but stories can flow from what might appear
minor issues. In 2003, a group of schoolgirls gained national publicity from their attempt to play football against boys.

The simplest way to find information from the courts is to turn
up. It sounds obvious, but many reporters seem to ignore the practice. They are happy to receive transcript and documents, which
they assume are at the fingertips of their court-reporting colleagues,
but they are hesitant to leave their offices. In this way they miss the
advantage of being known by the lawyers, legal officers and other
court staff. I make this point in Chapter 8, but it is worth saying it
here: court officials can be conservative. They want to know who
they are dealing with, and whether their trust will be abused when
they help the media. When they know they can trust reporters, they
are more likely to reward them with knowledge. The information
might be as basic as a hearing date, or a copy of a judgment or
sentencing remarks, but it is rare that a reporter will be worse off
for having made the effort.

The first place to look before heading to court is the court list.
Traditionally, at least one newspaper in a city will publish lists
of the higher courts. The lists will feature the names of the main
parties in cases, the court number, the starting time and the title and
surname of the judge. Remember to take identification. Security has
increased in the years since the September 11 attacks in the United
States. It is much more common for possessions to be scanned
at entrances to court buildings and to be checked by police when
extra security measures are set up for sensitive cases. Carrying a
media identification card can mean the difference between sitting
at seats set aside for journalists in a spot near the action and being
stuck at the back of the public gallery; in older court buildings, the
acoustics are challenging and the difference is noticeable. Most of
the higher courts have lists on their websites. Some will post them
to subscribers each day. While lists at Magistrates and Local courts

are generally available at the court building, distribution practices vary. They can be picked up at a court office, left for reporters at their press rooms or displayed on a wall. Reporters like to have a copy to carry with them so they can check names and charges as they work.

When one senior reporter in the 1980s saw me, a junior colleague, enthusiastically ticking court cases to check, he suggested an alternative method. If you speak with the clerks and the judges' associates, he said, you can find out something about the cases, and gradually cross them off your list. The ones you have left are the ones you check in court.

A current colleague has spent a lot of time trying to cultivate lawyers and police prosecutors who work regularly in the Magistrates court. If she is faced with a busy day and knows the contacts will be appearing in court, she telephones them to find out what they believe will happen. In that way she can plan her movements and if necessary organise other reporters. She knows there are many courts sitting at the same time. She cannot make a call and delay proceedings because she is running late or has to be somewhere else. The courts go on regardless. My colleague's system is not foolproof – an unexpected celebrity arrest or an application made at late notice can change the game plan – but it is a lot better than running from court to court in a panic.

The Australian court system has a number of 'flashpoints' which reporters can use to find stories. Practices vary between States and Territories – Tasmania does not allow reporting of bail applications, for instance – and between the criminal and civil law. Criminal prosecutions are aimed at behaviour that society or governments have decided to punish. Civil law deals mainly with infringements of rights. Individuals, companies and governments bring civil suits for claimed wrongs perpetrated by others, or breaches of contracts or duties. These are simple definitions, but many other publications and courses have been designed to examine the complexities of the different legal areas.

The criminal system

First appearance in court.   A person charged with an offence is usually brought to court to begin the legal process. Accused persons may be arrested and taken into custody, or charged by a document called a summons. The summons sets out the details of the charge and contains a date on which the accused is expected to appear at court. A magistrate will fix a further appearance date and often make arrangements with the prosecutor and defence lawyer about the future conduct of the case. A high-profile appearance could attract a lot of media attention. Reporters are bound by *sub judice* rules (see Chapters 3 and 4) but will seek details of the charge, personal details about the accused, and possibly a photograph which might be used immediately or kept as file footage for later use.

Bail application.   Even when the legal system is working well, a person charged with a serious crime might face several months, or more than a year, in jail while waiting for their case to be dealt with, or finalised. If prosecutors oppose bail, they will give the reasons briefly in open court. The defence side will try to modify the effect of those submissions and outline personal considerations which would justify restoring liberty to the accused. In this way, a summary of the allegations and defences can be described and reported. Be careful about prosecution evidence that details previous convictions or supposed confessions. Juries rarely hear evidence about an accused person's prior criminal history, and confessions are sometimes excluded from trials. They are prejudicial details that are often not reported until the end of a trial in a higher court.

Committal hearing.   Also known as a preliminary hearing, this procedure allows a magistrate to decide if there is prima facie (on the face of it, or at first sight) evidence which would allow a serious prosecution to be sent to a higher court. Defence counsel do not present their side of the argument but can test the prosecution case through cross-examination. Some lawyers are critical of media reporting being allowed at this stage of the process, because highly prejudicial evidence – sometimes not led at trial – can be aired in court. Reporting committals can be more difficult if the prosecutor does not make an opening statement to the magistrate. In that position, a court reporter is faced with trying to make a story from information revealed through questioning of witnesses. Another complication is the committal hearing run with hand-up briefs (documents given to the magistrate to examine before making a decision). Some State jurisdictions allow perusal or copying of materials put before the magistrate; where this is not allowed, reporting committals is more difficult.

Summary cases. Magistrates deal with less serious legal matters. They can set aside time to hear arguments and make a decision, reserve the decision, or hear it quickly among the list of cases placed before them in court. A trivial case can be just as newsworthy as a major prosecution. Good reporters keep their ears open in court as they wait for the hearing in which they are interested.

Arraignment. When a prosecution is sent to a higher court, the person facing the charges is asked to make a formal plea. A date for trial (not guilty plea) or pre-sentence submissions (guilty plea) is fixed. By this stage, the defence has had time to examine the material presented at the committal proceedings and make a decision about the progress of the matter. A guilty plea means the prosecution has been taken from the control of a jury, which would decide on the facts of the case, and given to a judge, who hears submissions and rules on penalty. Judges are perceived to be much less likely to be affected by news reports, which gives more leeway for mentioning details about the offending behaviour.

Trial. Assuming there are no suppression orders before a verdict is returned, you may report what is said in front of the jury. Lawyers and the judge often have discussions before and during a trial about admissible evidence and other issues. Unless the court has been closed, journalists can hear the arguments, but must not report them while the trial continues. Jurors hear controlled information. They are assumed to be judges of the facts, but are prone to influence from factors or information from outside the courtroom. In earlier times, they were asked not to speak with friends or family about the evidence or read, see or listen to news reports. Judges still give that advice, and now tell juries not to search for information on the internet. In 2004, as mentioned earlier, criminal trials in New South Wales were aborted, or stopped, when judges learned that jurors were conducting their own investigations. Information not put before the jury can be published after the trial, but reporters should check if suppression orders remain in force or whether a person convicted of a crime faces other charges to be dealt with in the near future.

Pre-sentence submissions and sentence.   The judge will hear submissions from defence counsel in mitigation of penalty, and from prosecutors about the seriousness of the offence. Witnesses can be called to give evidence about character, and the psychiatric or psychological makeup of the person facing sentence. Judges will often reserve their decision about penalty, which they will then present at a separate hearing. Many jurisdictions will publish sentencing remarks on paper or via the court website on the same day penalty is pronounced. Court reporters might see this as an advantage, but judges will increasingly look at the benefits. If they produce a penalty that attracts controversy, ordinary citizens can see the sentencing remarks – sometimes many pages long – and judge for themselves. Media representatives regularly use interviews with lobbyists or with victims or their families to criticise decisions that appear lenient. Public debate about decisions made on the community's behalf is obviously legitimate. But court reports should contain information from the decisions as well as criticism. I dislike it intensely when media organisations seek controversy by replacing material from court with opinion from every genius considered to have knowledge about a topic. Space and time for reports is limited, but it seems careless to feature comments without giving them a context. The trend explored on some media websites might be a solution. A link to the published sentence is placed next to the court report. Readers then can obtain information from a variety of sources.

Appeals.   Those convicted and sentenced can appeal against their finding of guilt and the penalty imposed on them. Prosecuting authorities can appeal against the leniency of a penalty. They can also challenge a decision to acquit in a legalistic sense. The finding of not guilty is not disturbed, but legal reasoning for the decision can be explored. The appeal launch, hearing and appeal court decision are set pieces which can yield stories. Hearings can be time-consuming and less accessible for writing because they are concerned with points of law rather than the evidence or facts of the case. Media outlets campaigning against prisoners' rights, for example, can point to appeals as an example of the outrageous demands placed on the public purse. Some appeals can seem trivial, but judges have reminded appellants that sentences can be increased as well as decreased. Appeal points, and whole appeals, have been abandoned at this point.

Special leave applications to the High Court, and the relatively few cases that make it to full argument before the country's highest legal tribunal, are the end of the legal process.

The civil system

Lodging the complaint. Law firms have become more adept at making the lodging of a complaint a public event. Solicitors bring paperwork to a court registry and provide copies of the documents they have just filed. It is better for the journalist to speak with and photograph the complainant, who has a personal interest in pursuing the court action. The encounter also provides pictures for use in the immediate publication and later in the process. Make an effort to seek the viewpoint of the other party; many will decline, some will make a token comment, but a few can give another perspective on the court fight. Be careful about court documents – they are not privileged until read in court (see Chapters 3 and 4). Reporters can later check the registry when the respondent files defences, but these can be filed as answers to previously numbered questions and are not necessarily illuminating.

Preliminary hearings. Many court hearings can take place between the start of a civil action and the final hearing. The dispute topic, number of witnesses, venue and validity of the complaint are often discussed before the matter is set down for trial. Complicating the process for the reporter is the possibility of settlement, which is sometimes confidential. In big cases, it is wise to keep in touch with the court official (associate or clerk) whose judicial officer is in charge of the case. Otherwise, the occasional telephone call to the lawyers in the case to check progress does not hurt.

Trial. It is common enough for civil cases to settle 'at the door of the court', or when a trial is about to start. Perhaps the respondent was trying to see if the complaint was pursued seriously, or the lawyers spotted the potential for bad publicity for a corporate client and alerted their representative to the presence of reporters in court.

Cases involving children as plaintiffs can require the approval of a judge, which means the issues are explained in court. It is a difficult balancing exercise when a judge or other court officer decides to suppress proceedings in the interests of the child. The action might have been a prominent one. It might have covered an issue of great concern to media audiences or the public at large. It is my experience that proprietors are not keen to risk a backlash by exposing a child to media scrutiny. They are more interested in making sure they do not lose the story.

Appeals.   Civil cases are subject to a similar appeals process to those in crime. Reporters can start their coverage on a previously unknown matter if they realise the significance of a civil appeal. Class actions or civil claims resulting from wrongdoing that affected diverse groups might become significant at the appeal court level.

Sitting in court

Courts are filled with customs and courtesies, but the most important is to be on time. Other areas of journalism might cope with lateness, but this one will not. Daily court reporters are slaves to the list. The publication of sentencing remarks and judgments, and better access to transcript, can help overcome the problem of absence from a hearing. But those who want to see the proceedings and describe the reactions of the parties involved have no choice: they must be at the courtroom when the case starts. Try setting your watch five minutes fast. That way, even regular latecomers have a fighting chance of being on time.

Dress respectfully. Jackets might be avoided in the summer heat, but men should wear a tie and women a smart blouse and trousers or skirt, or a good dress. Jeans and t-shirt are too informal, even if members of the public gallery or jurors can get away with it. On one occasion, I was asked at short notice to attend the swearing in of the new Chief Justice at Government House. Casual gear would not have helped that day.

You will notice judges and lawyers bow to each other as they enter and leave the court. It is manners to do so if you come in or go out during proceedings. Some judges will give you a small nod when they get to know you. Chewing gum, reading the paper, and drinking water, coffee, tea or fruit drinks are good ways of making court officials unhappy. They are very sensitive to the formality of the proceedings. Even if you do not share that view, they can be good long-term contacts, so it is wise to sacrifice comfort for the benefit of respect.

Mobile phones are annoying enough on public transport. They are hated in courts, and are distracting. Turn the telephone off, or leave it on silent mode in the courtroom. Some telephones have a very noisy 'silent' buzz and can be a source of constant worry for their owners, so check before you program the machine. The same principle applies to text messaging. Really, you should leave the courtroom to send them, but some reporters get away with it. Be very discreet. Some court officials would be happy to make sure you are not invited back in front of their judge or magistrate unless it was to answer a contempt charge for interfering with proceedings.

Practices vary, but it is wise to learn who is the accepted source for basic information such as ages, dates, addresses and charges. Prosecutors are often the source, but it might be that, as in Victoria for example, the prosecuting authorities are able to provide the details later by telephone. Make sure you introduce yourself properly. It is the polite and ethical thing to do, but it might also help those around the court to remember who you are. While obtaining details, check spellings and dates of birth rather than accepting an estimate.

Do not give barristers and judges the satisfaction of saying; 'They couldn't even spell my name right.' Check with associates and instructing solicitors. If you notice barristers wearing silk (shiny) robes, with or without a rosette on the back, it means they are a Queen's Counsel or Senior Counsel; ordinary barristers wear robes of humbler cloth. Ask your office to finance the purchase of a law diary, usually prepared by the law society or law institute in the local jurisdiction. If lawyers are happy to let you check details from their submission, do so. They speak a complicated version of English but you must write simply. Do not be afraid to ask basic questions. Lawyers appearing in a case have probably had months to familiarise themselves with the material they have presented in court; you might have heard it for the first time. Be cautious about interpretations that differ markedly from your notes – it is probably understandable that someone being quoted in the newspaper would like to have the best version of their submissions reported, rather than the accurate one.

What can we have?

An informal survey of court bureaucracies shows considerable variety across the country when it comes to giving reporters information. As a general rule, expect to pay to search and photocopy documents. Many jurisdictions allow access to written decisions; some appear to rely on the whim of judicial officers as to whether they are published at a convenient time, or at all. The tables below are summaries of information release practices across Australian courts. They cannot be completely comprehensive but are intended as a guide. The material was released in mid- to late 2004.

Table 2.1 Are copies of court judgments and sentencing remarks available?

NSW	Civil and criminal judgments from higher courts generally available on website. Local court sentencing remarks can be obtained rarely by special request. Some major local court decisions on internet.
Qld	Higher court judgments on website. Some sentences on website. Usually available same day. Magistrates Court not available.
Vic.	Yes in Supreme Court, though not always on same day as delivered. Common in County Court, sometimes in Magistrates Court.
SA	Sentencing remarks, inquest findings and judgments are published on-line. Usually same day, but not always.
WA	Judgments available on hard copy immediately. Sentences usually sent by email.
Tas.	Yes, often sent by email.
NT	Yes, except for sentencing remarks at the Magistrates Court. Otherwise, Supreme Court sentencing remarks and written judgments from all jurisdictions can be found on Supreme Court website within 24 hours.
ACT	Sentencing remarks and Supreme Court judgments generally on website same day and stay for 28 days.
Federal Court	Most available same day. Courts' media director sometimes emails judgments to media.
High Court	Judgments are on website half an hour after being delivered. They can be collected as hard copy in the Canberra registry. Locally relevant judgments received at High Court registries in NSW and Vic., and Supreme and Federal court in other jurisdictions.
Federal Magistrates Court	Many, but not all, are on website.
Family Court	Limited numbers of anonymised judgments are on website. Parties, witnesses or associated persons at proceedings cannot be identified.

Table 2.2 Can journalists get same-day transcripts of court proceedings?

NSW	Journalists can apply for transcript through reporting services branch of Attorney-General's department.
Qld	Yes, through State Reporting Bureau of Queensland.
Vic.	Yes.
SA	Yes, from the courts.
WA	Can get access, not copies, in criminal trials on judge's approval.
Tas.	Journalists can get access to transcript, but the court does not want to make it a habit.
NT	Free running transcript is available for all Supreme Court trials, and was made available at the Falconio case committal hearing. Otherwise, media can liaise with the NT court recording services.
ACT	Yes, but need to satisfy registrar and pay fee.
Federal Court	If the court or one of the parties has ordered it. A media rate can be negotiated.
High Court	Transcripts of appeal hearings usually available on website same evening. Special leave applications take a day or two.
Federal Magistrates Court	Parties can buy transcript. Journalists sometimes, in limited circumstances, can peruse court transcript.
Family Court	No.

Table 2.3 Can journalists get access to hand-up briefs at committal hearings?

NSW	No, but other rights exist regarding criminal files.
Qld	No, notes must be taken in court
Vic.	Yes, on approval from magistrate.
SA	Decision to be made by prosecuting authorities.
WA	No committal hearings.
Tas.	No.
NT	Requests had not been made, but probably would fall within the courts' access policy.
ACT	At the end of committal, notes can be taken from brief, but copying generally not allowed
Federal Court	N/A.
High Court	N/A.
Federal Magistrates Court	N/A.
Family Court	N/A.

Table 2.4 Can a) criminal or b) civil files be searched?

NSW	a) Non-party access is limited to pleadings and judgments in concluded proceedings. They include documents that record the result of a case, information from open court and material admitted into evidence. Scandalous, frivolous, vexatious, oppressive and irrelevant material may be struck out of documents. b) Media may inspect any document not suppressed or otherwise prohibited by law related to criminal proceedings to make a fair and accurate report. Access from start of proceedings until two days after the end.
Qld	a) & b) Yes.
Vic.	a) No. b) Yes in higher courts. Reporters must apply to magistrate in lower courts.
SA	a) & b) Journalists fill out a form to seek permission from judge to search.
WA	a) Yes, informal arrangements made in the interests of accurate reporting. b) Yes, under Supreme Court rules on same basis as members of public.
Tas.	a) Not before court hearing. b) Yes, limited access.
NT	a) Yes, in Magistrates Court. A registrar may require a written or oral justification. Not in Family Matters Court. b) Yes in Supreme Court.
ACT	a) & b) Yes, on reasonable grounds with current public interest.
Federal Court	a) & b) Yes, advance notice needs to be given for some migration cases.
High Court	Yes. Advance notice needs to be given for some migration cases.
Federal Magistrates Court	Yes, but leave to search will be given only to a person who has shown a proper interest for inspecting a judgment. Conditions may apply.
Family Court	No, unless you are a person with a proper interest and court permission.

New South Wales

Tape recorders and cameras are not permitted in New South Wales courts, but civil and criminal decisions, particularly in the higher courts, are published on the internet. Transcript costs are high, with minimum fees ranging from $64 to $75, but journalists can ask for a waiver. The general website <www.lawlink.nsw.gov.au> is the starting point for online information from the State's court system. Restrictions exist on searching civil files, with registrars referring

Table 2.5 Which parts of files can be examined?

NSW	Access in civil proceedings generally limited to judgments and pleadings in completed cases and material from open court. The media can inspect a wide range of criminal file documents from the start of the case until two days after the end.
Qld	All, except for material identifying juries or sealed by judicial officer.
Vic.	All, unless orders are made to seal parts of file. Court of Appeal criminal files cannot be examined.
SA	Generally, statements of claim, orders, affidavits and other information can be obtained, and exhibits photographed with permission.
WA	Criminal files: can arrange to inspect pleadings, exhibits and affidavits read in court; statements of material facts for sentencing; and appeal books.
Tas.	Criminal files available in open court can be searched after the hearing as an aid to the journalist. Pleadings can be searched, but no other documents.
NT	Criminal files: Permitted and prohibited public access to parts of files contained in *NT Law Almanac*. Most parts of civil files can be searched. File notes, reports and documents not in evidence cannot be searched in criminal files.
ACT	All, unless courts have sealed part of the file.
Federal Court	Affidavits not searchable unless admitted to court. Need to check location of file, as court has registries around the country.
High Court	Affidavits not searchable unless admitted to court. Need to check relevant registry for location of file.
Federal Magistrates Court	See restrictions above on leave to search files.
Family Court	Apart from the Attorney-General and a party in a case, other persons deemed to have a proper interest in the case or information from the court record may search a file.

'doubtful' access applications to the Chief Justice or another nominated judge. Assuming suppression orders or other legal bars do not exist, access to criminal files appears easier, provided it is attempted while the case is running or up to two days after it has finished. Court lists are posted on the internet, and at court buildings.

Queensland

Selected sentences from the higher courts (Supreme and District) are available on the Queensland courts website <http://courts.qld. gov.au> after the judge has revised them. Courts administration say

Table 2.6 What does it cost to copy and/or photocopy parts of files?

NSW	For depositions, transcript or diskette, minimum charge $64 to $75. Copying other documents costs $2 per page, with $10 minimum. Duplicate cassette $35.
Qld	Higher courts: usually $10.50 per file to search and $3 per page to copy with maximum $45 per document. Lower courts: $9 to $16 per file, $1.70 per page to copy
Vic.	Search fees $26 in Supreme Court if file number is known, $42 if not. Approx. $19 to $40 in County Court. Photocopying $1.50 per page.
SA	No cost for above access.
WA	Search fee $21. Photocopying $3 per page.
Tas.	Search fee $16. Photocopying document 50 cents per page.
NT	Supreme Court search fee $4, photocopying 60 cents to $1.20 per page, depending on whether court staff assist. Magistrates Court file inspection $10 per file; photocopying by court staff $1.20 per page.
ACT	Supreme Court $23 search fee, photocopying 20 cents per page. Fees regulations, i.e. regulations that set fees say that a videotape of a proceeding, or part of a proceeding costs $49, audio tape $39, CD-ROM $29, Floppy disc $15.
Federal Court	$13 per file search, $3 per page for photocopying.
High Court	$13 per file search, $3 per page for photocopying.
Federal Magistrates Court	Photocopying in Family Court matters 20–50 cents per page. Federal Court charges $4 for the first page and $1 per page after that.
Family Court	Photocopying 50 cents per page.

hard copies of judgments and sentences are usually available to journalists on the day they are delivered. On the website, judges choose sentences to be published according to their perceived significance or public interest. The remarks remain on the webpage for three months, then can be requested from the Supreme Court library. In November 2004, four Supreme Court and two District Court judges had placed sentencing remarks on the site. One Supreme Court judge provided 11 of 14 documents, while a District Court judge supplied all but one of the 19 available in that jurisdiction. Civil and criminal files can be searched in the higher and Magistrates courts. Journalists cannot tape-record in courtrooms, cannot obtain or copy the hand-up brief, and cameras are not permitted except on ceremonial occasions. Same-day transcripts can be obtained through the State Reporting Bureau of Queensland.

Victoria

Victorian Supreme Court judges generally have sentences and judgments ready for journalists on the day of delivery. An alternative measure for reporters is to tape-record the judge's remarks after signing an undertaking that the tape will not be used for broadcast. Same-day publication of written reasons is common, but not universal, in the County Court. Magistrates usually allow media access to decisions on the rare occasion that they are published after being reserved from an earlier date. Supreme Court decisions and sentences are published on the internet, but the court's media officer would like to see more on the same day. There are no formal rules about the use of still and video cameras, but informal arrangements have been made in crime and civil cases, usually at the start or end of a case. The judge's permission is required, and most of the filming has been performed in the Supreme Court. Civil files can be searched but criminal files are regarded as confidential. Basic facts about criminal proceedings, such as names, charges and the fact of an appeal being lodged, can be obtained. Reporters are not given access to Magistrates Court files but can apply for access to specific materials. They can submit a form for access to prosecution briefs at committal hearings and are permitted to make copies. Transcript is available in criminal trials and is normally emailed on the same day at no charge if a running transcript is being made. In civil cases, separate arrangements can be made, usually at a media rate, with commercial transcript providers. The Supreme Court website <www.supremecourt.vic.gov.au> contains links to other Victorian court websites.

South Australia

A suppression orders register lets the media and members of the public check on publication restrictions. But the onus is on the interested party to get the checks right – you will gain no sympathy if you miss an order. Complications could arise if a suppression order is lifted or lapses and notice is not given immediately. Sentencing remarks, inquest findings and judgments are published online, usually on the same day. South Australian links start at <www.courts.sa.gov.au>. Tape-recorders can be used in court as an aid to accuracy, not for broadcast; the tape must be erased within 48 hours. Judges can ask for tapes to be turned off while the court hearing is taking place. Still and video cameras are allowed for ceremonial sittings on a pool basis. Journalists must fill in forms and receive judicial permission to search files and court exhibits. Same-day transcripts can be obtained from the courts. News organisations are required to report subsequent acquittals or the dismissal of charges if they have published the name of any person accused of an offence. The acquittal report is to be given similar prominence to earlier coverage.

Western Australia

The WA media officer says that journalists can tape-record in courtrooms for the purpose of checking accuracy, not for broadcast, though this is not usually done in practice because transcript can also be checked if reporters have queries. The higher courts provide same-day access to transcript but no copies, usually after a two-hour 'turnaround'. Hard copies of sentences and judgments are provided immediately, while electronic access usually takes a couple of days. In big cases attracting public interest, such as the prosecution of Jack Roche under anti-terrorism laws, sentencing remarks are placed on the internet on the same day. The Supreme Court website <www.supremecourt.wa.gov.au> is a good starting point for queries. Magistrates refer bigger cases to the higher courts, but not through committal hearings. Daily lists are posted on the internet for the higher courts and provided in hard copy at the Magistrates Court for media organisations each day before court begins. Civil files can be searched for writs and statements of claim. Leave can be sought from courts or registrars for other documents. Informal arrangements can be made, in the interests of accurate reporting, for media representatives to inspect statements of material facts for sentencing, appeal books, and other material which has been read in court.

Tasmania

Judges provide copies of sentencing remarks by lunchtime for morning sentences and by 5 p.m. for afternoon hearings. Judgments are available as soon as they are delivered. Journalists are encouraged to receive these documents by email. Criminal files cannot be searched before hearings, only civil pleadings, but documents available in open court can be scrutinised after a hearing, usually as an aide-mémoire for the journalist. Court lists are published on government websites and a free email subscription list is available. Try <www.courts.tas.gov.au> as a starting point for information. Generally, cameras are allowed only in ceremonial sittings, but in important cases they have been used before the start of proceedings. A separate room with a large video screen broadcasting the court hearing was set up for the Martin Bryant (Port Arthur murders) case. Hand-up briefs cannot be obtained at the Magistrates Court, and only one transcript of proceedings is produced. Journalists cannot obtain transcript as of right, but court administrators can give them access to a copy if they have missed something. The administrators say they do not want to make a habit of that practice. There are no plans to appoint a courts media officer.

Australian Capital Territory

The ACT administration generally does not allow audio or video-taping in its courts or tribunals, sticking to the notion that only one transcript of court proceedings exists. Some exceptions have been made to the ban on cameras when there is strong public interest, mostly in coronial and other inquiries; file footage has been obtained in that way. Same-day transcript is available only when the court has ordered it to be prepared. Access to transcript varies between the Supreme and Magistrates courts, but registrars need to be satisfied that a proper reason has been given. ACT Supreme Court judgments and sentences are published on the site <www.courts.act.gov.au>, usually on the day they are delivered, and remain there for twenty-eight days. Journalists usually have access to complete files unless orders have been made sealing evidence. Publication is a different matter, and statutory restrictions exist on court dealings with children, domestic violence orders, jurors and protected witnesses, for example. The onus is on reporters not to publish protected information, but files are said to be clearly marked if they contain such material. Searches are allowed within a 'reasonable' period, while there is still perceived public interest in a case. Journalists can take notes from committal briefs but cannot copy them. Court lists are published on the website.

Northern Territory

The bible in the Northern Territory legal system is the *NT Law Almanac*, found on the government website and available on compact disc for $10. It contains information access policies for all Territorian courts, and other details about the system. Expect to see written judgments and Supreme Court sentences on the web within 24 hours at <http://www.nt.gov.au>. Court lists are found on the same site by 4 p.m. each day, and free running transcript is available for all Supreme Court criminal trials. It was also provided for the committal hearing of Bradley John Murdoch, who was charged with murdering British backpacker Peter Falconio. The media interest in the case, particularly from the United Kingdom, prompted specific action from the NT Director of Public Prosecutions. Letters, maps and media updates were prepared to ensure the smooth running of the legal proceedings. See more discussion in Chapters 3 and 4. Magistrates Court sentences are not published; journalists have apparently not requested copies of hand-up briefs (documents outlining the prosecution case in a committal hearing) and the government is considering whether to appoint a full-time media officer after using one for the Murdoch matter.

Federal Court and Federal Magistrates Court

Few requests are made for transcript, but paperwork exists, downloadable from <www.fedcourt.gov.au>, which also links to the Federal Magistrates Court site. The court has regularly recorded for television and radio broadcasts, usually from technology at a centralised location, rather than having a number of tape-recorders lined up on the judicial bench. Most judgments are available on the internet the same day, and the court's media director will sometimes send them to reporters by email. File searches are limited to statements of claim and other basic paperwork before a hearing starts. Applications for affidavits must be made to the judge hearing the case. Court lists are published on the homepage late on the day before and can be mailed out; transcripts must be requested from commercial providers. The Federal Court has started an e-court through its website allowing case searches online. A trip to the court registry is necessary to search documents, but some of the basics can be obtained through the new access. The Federal Magistrates Court requires judicial leave for audio recording and is restricted in what it can allow in cases dealing with family and migration matters. As a general rule, cameras are not permitted but file searches are allowed. As discussed below under the Family Court section, leave must be sought to search files in those matters and will be allowed only for those showing a proper interest. In limited cases, journalists can ask to peruse, but not copy, the court's transcript in the registry.

High Court

Proceedings in this court cannot be tape-recorded. Cameras are allowed on ceremonial occasions by arrangement well ahead of time with the media officer. Usually, this is done on a pool basis, which means the network allowed to film must make footage available to its competitors. Aside from a 1998 documentary on the court, cameras have not been permitted for hearings. All of the judges, parties and lawyers in a case would have to agree for filming to take place. Good luck.

Judgments are published on the website <www.hcourt.gov.au> within about 30 minutes of the decision being announced in court. One-page judgment summaries are on the site soon after and are emailed to a media distribution list. Copies are held at the Canberra registry, and if the case is a New South Wales or Victorian one, also at the counter of either of those registries. In other capital cities, the Federal or Supreme Courts provide registry services, and the judgments are collectable the following day. The High Court website holds copies of judgments dating back to 1947. Generally court files can be searched, but affidavits must have been formally admitted into court to be seen. Requests to search can be made by email or fax, but the speed of searching can be determined by the file location. The Canberra registry holds files for cases starting in the Australian Capital Territory, Northern Territory, Western Australia and Queensland. The Sydney office has files for New South Wales only, and Melbourne has Victorian, South Australian and Tasmanian files. The paperwork is transferred to Canberra a week or two before appeal hearings and may remain there afterwards for some time. Communication with the Canberra registry before a planned search to check on the file location can save time. Court lists are on the website, as are transcripts of appeal hearings. Appeal transcripts are posted late on the day of the hearing, but chambers and special leave application transcripts might take a couple of days after checking.

Family Court

Publication of information is restricted under Family Court rules. Video and photographic images cannot be published, and those involved in proceedings cannot be identified. Selected and anonymised judgments are available on the court's website, <www.familycourt.gov.au>, but files cannot be searched unless the searcher is deemed to have a proper interest; transcripts are not provided and tape-recording is not allowed. The exception to the publicity restrictions is activated when a child goes missing, often when a parent fails to return with the child after a contact visit. In those cases, names, personal details and photographs are released and placed on the court's webpage in an effort to locate the missing child. The court may make a publication order allowing publicity for that purpose. In one case on the website, a media release was included, but outlets were urged not to change the wording to make sure they did not breach the provisions of the specific order. Court lists are on the website, daily newspapers and noticeboards at registries.

Chapter 3

Contempt

The legal system operates on the assumption that it is open to the public. Thinkers, judges and lawyers have argued this principle for hundreds of years. It means that members of the public have the right to see how justice is administered in their name. The US Supreme Court, in a decision on public trial rights, recognised that its open trial system, like ours, came from English common law. The court noted that public trials were said to have been firmly established by the 17th century, and suggested that public trials were part of the system long before rights we would consider rudimentary today, such as calling witnesses, having legal counsel, the ability to prepare a defence, and having prior notice of charges or prosecution evidence.

Commentators use pragmatic and theoretical justifications for public hearings: perjury might be deterred because others (presumably including those with knowledge of the issue before court) could hear the evidence; judges would be dissuaded from abuse of their positions; and the community could be confident in the integrity and impartiality of courts because their practices were open to scrutiny. As one judge has suggested, the fact that courts were held openly rather than secretly was an essential part of their character and distinguished them from the work of administrative officials. Jurors hear similar statements when they are discharged after finishing their work – community members decide on trials in open court, as opposed to anonymous officials in other systems.

In 2004, the Victorian Court of Appeal reaffirmed the open court principle in deciding whether suppression orders should continue on police investigative practices then being kept from the general public. The suppression order was overturned, a decision confirmed later at the High Court. At the time of writing, the High Court's written reasons for the judgment have not been published. Media and other interested parties anticipate significant opinions from the court about suppression orders. Anyone interested in the topic will be keen to read the decision.

The three Victorian judges supported the idea that the administration of justice might be corrupted if the operation of courts was not on public view. Ordinarily, they said, the media should be entitled to communicate to the public what it has a right to hear and see. The Full Federal Court in 1995 saw a practical side to media reporting: few members of the public had the time or inclination to attend court in person, so the open court principle demanded the media be free to report what took place. The judges in that court can be taken to have recognised some of the basic elements of daily life: citizens work, they care for family members, some of them will have no concern about the way justice works.

Quite apart from that, there is limited space in a courtroom. Most would accommodate fewer than a hundred seats in the public gallery, and in high-profile cases some of them are occupied by court staff and barristers. When some lawyers speak dismissively about the inconvenience of having the media in courts, it is tempting to campaign for an Open Courts Week, in which the public would be invited to turn up en masse and demand their right to see justice in action. The system would struggle to cope, and the delays caused by the pressure on resources would make the exercise counterproductive. However, it might show some why it is important to communicate to the wider community.

But there are competing interests. In 1999, the British Lord Chancellor, Lord Irvine of Lairg, gave a speech about courts and the media. He said the first and fundamental purpose of every court was to deliver justice according to law; the right to public access was secondary to that purpose. The courts had to show that excluding the public was necessary in serving justice – that justice could not be done without the exclusion.

The law of contempt of court regulates some of those exclusions. Another fundamental legal principle is that everyone is entitled to a fair trial. Justice James Spigelman, the NSW Chief Justice, outlined the principle in a 2003 lecture. The courts would not tolerate trials being conducted in an illegal or improper way. An accused person could normally expect competent legal representation, an interpreter when needed, and to know the case he or she had to meet. Debate about separate trials could be expected when more than one person was charged. Prosecutors were obliged to put their case fully and fairly. Judges should be impartial, avoid intervening too much during the trial, and help unrepresented litigants enough to make sure the proceedings were fair. Judges had to be wary of prejudicial evidence such as previous convictions, alleged bad behaviour, or purported identification by witnesses.

A British legal text (Arlidge et al. 1999) asserts that punishment has been delivered since about 1250 for interfering with legal proceedings. The early contempts included assaults, verbal abuse and disobedience. By the 18th century, the press and pamphleteers were punished for publishing material said to interfere with the administration of justice. In 1821, according to another text on contempt, a newspaper was fined £500 for publishing a court report when a judge made orders delaying publication until a number of treason trials had finished.

What does this mean for modern journalists? The fair trial concept has another basic requirement: a person is innocent until proved guilty. In practical terms, jurors are expected to make their decisions on the material they hear in court. Details of previous convictions, or an accused's purported bad character, are for this reason regularly excluded from criminal trials. Jurors are warned not to search the internet, read media reports, or speak with family and friends while the trial is continuing. It is easy to see what impact this might have on commercial media proprietors who rely on attracting audiences – to attract advertisers in turn – in order to make money. Lord Irvine described the media as acting *for* the public, but not being the same *as* the public.

Inevitably, all forms of media reporting involve some editorial process, a selective filter which chooses and shapes what it reports. That process of filtration is increasingly subjected to market pressures. News is a commodity, with a cash value attached.

It is obvious, for instance, that media outlets would love to report that a convicted murderer was facing trial again for murder. But legal advocates would argue that this is exactly the sort of information that could prejudice juries. 'If he did it once, why wouldn't he do it again?' the jurors might ask, while ignoring important evidence. When judges and lawyers talk about balancing competing interests between a free press and a fair trial, this is the sort of issue they are talking about. It is also a consideration in discussing the central form of contempt faced by court reporters – sub judice contempt.

Sub judice means 'under judicial consideration'. Its restrictions apply when a case is pending or awaiting resolution. In criminal proceedings, this is from the time a summons or warrant for arrest is issued until acquittal or the end of the appeal process. In a civil case, the rules exist from the issuing of a writ, statement of claim or summons until the appeal process has ended. The start of a police investigation does not mean proceedings are pending, so you can publish whatever information you receive provided an arrest is not imminent.

But be careful about defamation – accusations about a person do not have special status because police have made them. Also be careful about publishing if it is likely that a warrant or summons will be issued between the time of obtaining information and publishing. Some lawyers suggest that it is wise to assume the proceedings are pending from the start in cases where police would know who was likely to be arrested. Whichever policy is adopted, it is irrelevant whether you intended to commit contempt. The rule applies to publication of material that tends to affect the public administration of justice in a practical way, and here intent to harm is not a factor. The NSW and WA law reform commissions have investigated the question of intent and the lack of a maximum penalty for contempt, but political change might be some time away.

Before we talk about the sorts of information that should not be published, some observations from the coalface should be considered. Colleagues attending media law discussions will protest that the restrictions being suggested for them by lawyers do not apply in real life. Here is an example. It is fairly common at the end of a criminal trial for feature articles to be written summarising the prosecution and defence arguments, and sometimes revealing information that was not before the jury. Sometimes this information was not even before the court but was uncovered by a journalist's inquiries. Clearly, the court process is continuing, but the information is published on the basis that judges, through their legal training, are perceived by the law to be much less susceptible than jurors to prejudicial material. A cautious lawyer might advise not to publish. In practice, it happens often.

Journalists have been active in interviewing witnesses and suspects after a crime has been committed and before an arrest has been made. In some of the underworld killing cases in Victoria, supposed criminal links of accused people and reports about their behaviour have been made after charges were laid. Reporting is seen to be pushing the boundaries of what is allowable under contempt of court rules. Prosecuting perceived breaches might be a two-edged sword. If flaws are found in the technical process of bringing a contempt action or a clever defence succeeds, the media might achieve more freedom in reporting during the sub judice period.

At a 2004 contempt seminar, an unnamed newspaper executive was said to have declared that he did not know what the rules were any more. Material was being published that would never have been seen in the past, for example the names of suspects, and apparently media investigations were being conducted while a case was proceeding. At that stage, contempt prosecutions for the adventurous publications were being investigated but had not been issued. Was the law being taken in directions that had not been contemplated in Australia? One judge advances the theory that publishing under threat of contempt is like a pendulum. Media outlets, emboldened by previous recent success in avoiding prosecution, take it just a little bit further. Their competitors respond because they want to keep up in a competitive market. The practice becomes established, or it is extended again. Then a contempt prosecution is launched and succeeds. The media companies are fined – it can be an expensive day out when the fines and legal costs are combined – and executives become more nervous about wasting money. So a more conservative policy is adopted until the next big case.

It is not a bad theory, but it requires a bit of organisation by the media companies. They need competent and aggressive media lawyers to know when to publish and when to back off. It is not an exercise for amateurs, or those starting their careers. Contempt of court fines can cost tens of thousands of dollars. Legal costs are also prohibitive. It is safer and cheaper to follow the sub judice rules. If a media company wants to challenge them, it will not leave the decisions to a junior reporter.

Caution might be the best policy, in the absence of specific legal advice, but courts also treat juries as being pretty robust. They have to, otherwise why would they have criminal jury trials unless they assumed the jurors would act on the evidence and directions by the trial judge? That is the paraphrased view of one judge in an appeal hearing. The then Australian Chief Justice, Sir Anthony Mason, and Justice John Toohey said in another appeal that the mere possibility that a juror might have learned of a prior conviction was not enough to conclude that a miscarriage of justice had occurred. It was inherently possible in a criminal trial, they said, that jurors might acquire irrelevant and prejudicial information. In a Canadian case, a judge said it would be naive to think it would be possible, in an age of rapid news dissemination, to select twelve jurors who had heard nothing of a notorious case. Jurors could give a true verdict according to the evidence even if they had prior knowledge, or a tentative opinion, about the case.

In a study of New South Wales criminal jury trials, researchers reported that a large majority of jurors rejected the notion that publicity had any effect on their perception of the case, or their decision. A significant majority said they did not believe publicity had influenced other jurors. They discussed media reports in the jury room and found them inaccurate or inadequate in a number of respects. Some jurors suggested newspaper reports were usually a 'load of crap', made it look like the reporter was covering another trial, or that coverage by one newspaper was the 'comic relief of the day'.

Such views do not constitute an invitation to reporters to go for broke during criminal prosecutions. It should tell them that it is possible to tell stories within the contempt restrictions, but that subtlety is required. Below are the general rules that reporters should follow. Compare them with Australian contempt cases and penalties listed by the NSW Law Reform Commission.

You can report the bare facts about a case. This may include general details about an offence, such as the fact of a body being found in a homicide case, the name of a victim, unless it is suppressed (for example in a sexual assault matter), if police are continuing investigations, and other facts not to be contested at trial. At an early stage, it is difficult to tell what will be contested. This is an area in which media organisations have been more aggressive than traditional advice would suggest.

The coverage of the capture and arrest of Martin Bryant over the Port Arthur murders, the Wales-King and underworld killings cases in Victoria and the disappearance of British tourist Peter Falconio and subsequent charging of Bradley John Murdoch expanded on the details usually published in the sub judice period. None of these stories would have been reported without legal advice.

When big cases arise, media outlets are careful to make sure they take calculated risks, if they need to take risks at all. Sticking to the 'bare facts' philosophy will avoid problems in the other 95 per cent of cases.

Avoid publishing an accused person's previous criminal record, or indirect references, like 'notorious prisoner' or 'underworld hitman'. Do not publish witness accounts, anything that might identify the accused, if identity is likely to be an issue at trial, or material that might sway a jury for or against the person charged. In reality, media outlets now try to interview witnesses before anyone is charged, so they are not offending the sub judice principle. Photographs can be a difficult matter. Generally they will not be published when identity is an issue, but they might be when it is clear, for example, that a person has killed but the dispute is whether the offence is murder or manslaughter. When photographs are taken, judges do not want to see published pictures of an accused in handcuffs, which indicates he or she is in custody. Careful cropping of a photograph can eliminate that problem, but experience suggests it is wise to remind subeditors. Fundamentals can be forgotten in the excitement of placing a strong image on a prominent newspaper page. Reports made during proceedings should not comment on the merits of a prosecution or suggest a person should be convicted or acquitted.

A simple sub judice rule: do not talk to jurors. Broadcasters have got into trouble by talking to jurors on air, but the more common encounter is around the court building. Judges tell juries they should not talk to anyone they see in the court precinct, especially someone they recognise from the trial in which they are sitting. The courts are very concerned about the reality, or appearance, that a person connected with a hearing could influence the jury's decision. Even a simple 'hello' can be reported back to the judge, so it is good policy to look straight ahead and walk past if you see jury members inside or outside the premises.

I try to make sure I am not swapping theories about a case in the court corridors or anywhere jurors might be sitting. Beware the cafés around the court building. Keep the pressroom door closed if you are discussing a prosecution or a civil case involving a jury. It takes time and costs money if a trial has to start again. Jurors should not be identified. Some jurisdictions allow interviews with them without identification and with their consent, but that is definitely a time when the lawyers should be called. Likewise, the media in News South Wales, Queensland and Victoria may not seek information from a juror or publish juror deliberations. Publishing deliberations may be contempt of court in other jurisdictions.

The time and extent of publication can influence decisions about using potentially prejudicial material. In the Victorian Supreme Court in 2004, media lawyers used the 'six-month' rule in opposing a suppression order placed on material in a criminal prosecution. They relied on a ruling from the 1990s in which another judge considered it unlikely that jurors would be prejudiced by media dissemination of some evidence when a trial in the case was at least six months away. The judge in the 2004 case did not accept there was such a rule but said there was strong argument to suggest that the passing of time would limit the impact of publicity. Again, this was a case where lawyers carefully scrutinised the court stories being written. Do not assume you can publish anything you want because an anticipated trial is not scheduled for months.

Court stories published in the big daily newspapers or on metropolitan television and radio will obviously attract big audiences. Certainly, the owners hope they will. The audience will be multiplied if the story is then published interstate, but that creates its own dangers with contempt. Some newspapers, when covering a major trial, will prepare different accounts for publication in different States. For example, a trial is being held in South Australia and is being covered by Victorian newspapers, which send early editions to South Australia for sale. Prejudicial material which might be presumed to affect potential jurors would be cut out of the South Australian edition but included in following editions distributed locally. One newspaper, not from either State, tried that policy but had different names for each edition. Confusion arose when the edition names changed and a story intended for local consumption found its way into the interstate edition. An apology solved the problem, but the consequences could have been worse. A similar effect could be felt in a local publication. Trials are often held in the community in which an offence is said to have been committed. Court staff say judges are going 'on circuit'. They may hear a number of different cases – criminal and civil – in a rural city or large town. The cases will concern matters from the local area and juries will be drawn from that population. Publishing prejudicial stories in the local paper could then have a big effect because they were directed at the limited population from which jurors would be drawn.

Fair and accurate reports of proceedings in open court are allowed. That means you cannot report suppressed material, evidence raised in a closed court (you will probably be booted out of the courtroom, anyway) or pre-trial proceedings conducted in the absence of the jury (usually called a *voir dire* hearing).

A pre-trial proceedings hearing usually deals with the admissibility of evidence. In a big case, reporters often take notes from pre-trial argument for use after the trial. Reports from the trial must be clear and unbiased and must substantially represent what occurred in court. If the day's hearing mainly represented the prosecution case, make sure readers know an accused has pleaded not guilty, or a civil defendant has denied liability. The report should avoid commentary and should be published fairly soon after the hearing. A daily newspaper would normally expect to report the day after the hearing, a weekly paper the week after. Describe the charges accurately and make it clear to readers or audiences if a witness or accused has denied an allegation made against them. It is common to name the lawyers, the judge and the court in which the proceeding is being held, and to say if the case is continuing or has been adjourned.

Anyone involved in court proceedings cannot be subjected to improper pressure. The pressure might be directed at making a litigant settle or drop a case, or a witness not to testify or to change evidence. The media could be at risk by publishing threats or mis-representing the parties' involvement.

Avoid publishing comment or other material from outside court during a trial. New South Wales and Victorian judgments from the late 1990s make it clear that the media have to be very careful about making comments that go beyond a fair and accurate report. The publishers of *The Australian* newspaper and business journalist Mark Westfield were fined for contempt over comments Mr Westfield made while a criminal trial was being heard. In a separate prosecution, Sydney radio station 2UE and broadcaster John Laws were fined and ordered to share court costs regarding comments made during a murder trial, which had to be aborted. During the Westfield contempt case, Justice Bill Gillard summed up the rule: 'Once a matter is before the courts, you do not comment. It is as simple as that.' When handing down his decision, he added: 'Our system is trial by jury, not trial by media. Every accused has the right to a fair trial, no matter how unpopular his cause may appear to be.'

Journalists can criticise judges and their decisions, but the courts tend to draw the line when the criticism includes allegations of corruption or bias. This category is known as scandalising the court, or saying or doing something that undermines public confidence in the court system. You would imagine that a journalist with real evidence of corruption or bias would make sure the evidence would stand up in court. High Court Justice Michael Kirby has argued that scandalising the court was used occasionally in the past to punish journalists deemed to have crossed the line of permissible criticism. But he said the law appeared to have been cut back in Australia, and criticism of the judiciary had become, in some ways, part of popular entertainment. He said judges had been rendered accountable to the tabloids, and named politicians and talkback radio hosts as other attackers.

Sydney Morning Herald journalist Paul Sheehan has criticised judicial decisions in his home State, but quotes from judgments and presents reasons why he believes those judgments were incorrect. In one article, 'The contempt is mutual, your Honour', published in March 2004, Mr Sheehan is blunt in his criticism of a majority appeal court decision in a rape case. He comments on and contradicts the judges, using his observations and purported conduct of others as the basis for his views. He even sympathises with the constraints placed on judges by legal precedent.

His approach contrasts with that of the late union leader Norm Gallagher, who was jailed for three months for suggesting he was able to appeal successfully against a contempt conviction because the appeal court judges bowed to union power. Nevertheless, some behaviour has been deemed insulting but not scandalising. A Victorian solicitor has been found not to be in contempt of court when he said (away from the court) that a judge 'has got his hand on his dick' when he granted an injunction that did not suit the lawyer.

Courts may find there is no contempt of court if prejudicial material was an incidental by-product of discussions about matters of public concern. In other words, the importance of that discussion might outweigh an individual's right to a fair trial. You would be correct in thinking that such a case is rare. The principle is based on a 1937 action that related to the Sydney *Truth* newspaper's allegations that a group of master bakers – associated under a company called Bread Manufacturers Ltd – were acting to keep bread prices high. The relevant articles were published after a writ had been issued by a bread carter against Bread Manufacturers Ltd. The newspaper was prosecuted for contempt, but the judge found in its favour. He said the discussion of public affairs or denunciation of public abuses could not be required to be suspended because there might be some prejudice to a litigant as an unintended by-product. The successful application is rare. Broadcaster Derryn Hinch failed in an attempt to rely on it when charged with contempt after a broadcast that criticised a man with previous criminal convictions and facing sexual assault charges who was in charge of a youth organisation.

Contempt can apply to the way you behave in court. (Some indication of proper behaviour has been given in Chapter 2.)

Reporters have been ordered from court for reading newspapers and magazines (they held them indiscreetly above the desk) and once in my presence for grinning as the prosecutor began his opening address in a murder trial. There were extenuating circumstances in that case – an opaque window at the top of the courtroom wall showed someone in an upstairs room moving about and arranging furniture, apparently oblivious to the serious events below. On that occasion, I was happy to give the unfortunate reporter the information he missed.

Needless to say, the careless use of another reporter's notes for your story is fraught with risk. Some journalists have relied on the practice. They appear to have been lazy, or to have trusted the other reporter more than themselves.

It is fairly unusual to see media representatives, or members of the public, facing penalty for contempt in the face of the court, as bad behaviour in the courtroom is known. Noisy mobile phones attract admonishment or stares from the judicial bench. Many court officials are proactive in warning about drinking water, wearing hats, and other affronts to the dignity of the occasion. The worst damage journalists generally do to themselves is to their reputation. Those who work around the courts know how seriously they have to take the legal process. They are much less likely to trust you if they think you are treating it as a joke.

If there are rules governing or preventing the use of tape-recorders, for example, follow them and the surrounding bureaucracy. Many judges will give you the benefit of the doubt – if you have checked beforehand and someone has forgotten to bring the appropriate signed document to court, they will allow taping and sort out the paperwork later. But some see departure from formality as a challenge to their authority. In those situations there is no point arguing if the likely result is a warm inner glow and a ban on using the recorder. Sort out what you need and attack the wider problem later.

Courts and tribunals have powers to demand information. They can ask parties in cases to exchange information with each other and call for witnesses to provide evidence or produce documents. Witnesses must answer questions asked of them in court. Barristers can complain to the judicial officer hearing a case if they believe the answer is non-responsive or not forthcoming. By making and enforcing demands for information, the court can do justice based on all available and relevant material. Refusal to comply, or hiding or destroying information sought by the court, can be punished as contempt of court.

Attached to this power is a major source of conflict between journalism and the law. Journalists may be given privileges in court but are regarded as having no special rights over those of ordinary citizens. If a judge asks for the source of information for a story, the reporter is compelled by law to comply. Journalists have been jailed and fined for refusing, which they may do out of respect for their code of ethics. Clause 3 of this code sets out the requirements regarding sources.

> Aim to attribute information to its source. Where a source seeks anonymity, do not agree without first considering the source's motives and any alternative attributable source. Where confidences are accepted, respect them in all circumstances.

The clause gives good advice, apart from urging journalists to respect the confidentiality of their sources. In effect, it warns them to be slow to accept a condition of anonymity for a source: examine their motives, look for alternative attributable sources. I would add, 'Be wary about background information or briefings'. Receiving material for background, not attribution, can mean that all the interesting information is provided with no promise by the source to take responsibility for it.

An attempted interview with a solicitor ended unhappily one day after we disagreed about the nature of our chat. He wanted to give only background details, with no 'on the record' questions and nothing to be written to connect him with the published details. I wanted to be able to ask questions on the record and was happy to signal when that would be. 'Sorry, I can't help you,' he replied. As it happened, I got what I needed from another member of the legal team acting for the same client. But I am sure I would have received little support from my original contact had there been any trouble and a court wanted me to reveal my source.

In most cases, court reporters should not encounter trouble about sources. We work in a public venue and make a point of trying to disclose correctly the information sources in our stories.

Sometimes the story can look dull when almost every paragraph is attributed, but you can be sure to receive telephone calls from subeditors if the position is not clear. Attribution is part of accuracy in court stories – it lets readers know we were at court, and we are happy to be specific about who said what. Attribution could be an issue when contacts have gone out of their way to help you or give you information. Reporters interviewing political activist Albert Langer outside court in 1996 were asked to supply notes and tapes, because the interview and pamphlets he was handing out were relevant for further contempt proceedings. Some handed over the material quickly, others sought legal help to oppose. All were unhappy that they were made part of the process.

Contempt penalties have ranged from a finding of fault to fines of $200 000, and imprisonment when journalists refused to reveal sources. The NSW Law Reform Commission in 2003 listed penalties for sub judice contempt in Australia since 1980. As reported in the *Sydney Morning Herald*, five media organisations were fined a total of $670 000 for their publications stemming from the arrest of Paul Gerald Mason, 28, for three murders and an attempted murder in 1989. The *Herald* story said media outlets reported that Mason was said to have confessed to police. One television channel broadcast an interview with Mason and an interview with a police officer to the effect that Mason had confessed. The contempt prosecutions continued despite Mason's suicide while he was on remand. Other substantial penalties were imposed for publishing former NSW Premier Neville Wran's statement expressing his belief in the inno-cence of Justice Lionel Murphy; a television broadcast just before a committal hearing involving Justice Murphy; and the publication of photographs of Ivan Milat, then accused of the 'backpacker' murders. Newspapers were punished consistently for mentioning previous convictions of accused persons facing other charges. They were also fined for calling an accused a 'prison escapee' or 'danger-ous criminal' during the court process.

If a publication has been found to be in contempt, courts will consider its seriousness and its effect on proceedings. They will look at the language used, the type of publication, the audience size, and the length of time between publication and the trial. Media outlets keen to minimise penalty will point to their contrition, be open about the offence and point to improvements made since to their system of checks and balances designed to prevent the offence. Proprietors tend to be fined more than reporters or broadcasters, but reporters have been ordered to pay $10 000 and more after being found guilty.

In 1999, media lawyer Peter Bartlett prepared a checklist for reporters concerned about contempt of court. It asks a series of questions, based on the common contempt issues surrounding court reports. Journalists were asked to answer 'Yes' or 'No', or supply other specific information. I reproduce it here as a guide.

Q. Is there a case pending in relation to this article? (A case is pending if charges have been laid in a criminal case up until the final appeal is heard, and in a civil case once a writ has been issued up until the last appeal is heard.)

A. Yes.
   No.

Q. When is the case listed for hearing?

A. Now.
   Listed for ...

Q. Is the case being heard by a judge, a magistrate or a jury?

A. Judge.
   Magistrate.
   Jury.

Q. Has a suppression order been made in relation to anything in the article?

A. Yes.
   No.

Q. Is any of the material in the article prohibited from publication by legislation?

A. Yes.
   No.

Q. Is the story a fair and accurate report of the evidence given in the case? (i.e. no discussion of evidence given in the absence of the jury, evidence disallowed or questions disallowed).

A. Yes.
   No.

Q. Has the guilt or innocence of the accused been presupposed in the article? (e.g. Are the accused's prior convictions reported or are prejudicial information, confessions or identifying photographs of the accused published?)

A. Yes.

No.

Q. Does the article attack the credibility of a witness of a victim?

A. Yes.

No.

Q. Has a jury deliberation been discussed in the article?

A. Yes.

No.

Q. Does the article identify a juror or the case the juror is involved in?

A. Yes.

No.

Q. Does the article unfairly criticise the counsel or judiciary involved? (e.g. accusations of bias, personal attacks).

A. Yes.

No.

Chapter 4

Defamation

A father sues after a newspaper reports that he, not his son, is facing trial over a robbery. Another publication faces a $2.5 million damages award after it publishes defamatory material from a leaked affidavit that was not read in open court. An article critical of a magistrate is criticised by an appeal court for failing to fairly and accurately report the facts. The piece costs $246 500 in damages and many thousands of dollars in legal fees.

It is correct, as a former colleague suggested, that court reporters face many more concerns about contempt of court than they do about defamation. They are also more likely to be covering defamation cases than appearing in them. A State premier, policemen, broadcasters, businesspeople, lawyers, doctors, sportspeople, newspapers and an actor have been some of the parties in defamation cases in my experience. A fair and accurate report of court proceedings, as we have discussed, carries a qualified privilege against being sued for publishing defamatory evidence or statements that are made in legal proceedings. The authors of the statements receive an absolute privilege to make them in open court, so that the pursuit of justice is not shackled.

Defamation law lets individuals and companies take action to redress damage to their reputations. Material is said to be defamatory if imputations, or meanings, that are found in it, including inferences, injure the reputation. Injury can be caused if the subject is:

- exposed to hatred, contempt or ridicule
- lowered in the estimation of right-minded observers
- shunned or avoided as a result.

According to Freeman (1994), defamation is often unintentional, but that is irrelevant to the law. She says it does not matter what the publisher intended to say; it is what can be read into the words that counts. Armstrong and colleagues (1995) say the law operates on the meanings that ordinary viewers, listeners or readers – as hypothetical referees – would give them. They agree that the meaning intended by the publisher or understood by the intended audience does not matter. The law recognises the natural and ordinary meaning of words, and beyond that special meanings or innuendos. It could be defamatory to state that a moral crusader regularly visited premises not named in the publication but understood by some to be a brothel or illegal gambling den. Those who had extra knowledge about the premises could bring a different meaning to the words. The crusader could be seen to be immoral for visiting the address or a hypocrite for preaching one thing and apparently doing another. The natural and ordinary meaning of the words would be considered in the context in which they were published and the general background at the time of publication.

The media law guide for my employer recommends that journalists should look at stories from the audience's viewpoint. Could an ordinary, reasonable reader look at your publication in a way other than you intended? It suggests a good rule of thumb: if you would not want others to say a certain thing about you, the chances are that it is defamatory. Watch for the context in which remarks are made, the combination of images and text, the use of rumours, humour and jargon. One media lecturer suggested that journalists should have dirty minds. He meant that they could pick mistakes or hidden meanings in copy because they had knowledge of colloquial expressions. An obvious example would be the different meaning for the word 'thong'. In Australia, thongs have been the name given to a form of beach footwear, but in other countries the word describes skimpy underwear, otherwise called g-strings. Columnists have had fun with the confusion – one reported a visitor being concerned that officials would check if patrons at a sporting event were wearing thongs. Locals generally would understand the reference, but the term has a hidden meaning to another audience. This reporter has been corrected a couple of times when referring to thongs. The listeners on those occasions preferred another colloquial term, flip-flops, to describe the footwear.

Defamation can occur through two types of publication. Slander is the spoken form of a defamatory statement and libel is defamation in a permanent form. In an action for slander, a plaintiff would have to prove monetary loss, while in a libel action it would be necessary to prove only that the plaintiff had been defamed. Publication of defamatory material could occur through a conversation, a fax or email, electronic broadcast or internet transmission. All involved in the process may be liable if they report the material, even if they do not say they agree with it. Defamatory radio and television broadcasts are regarded as libel. A person can sue for defamation successfully if they can prove:

- the information was published to at least one other person
- it contained defamatory material
- the defamatory publication was about the person or company now taking the action.

Defamation rules vary in Australia's States and Territories. The State governments and federal government in 2004 have revived debate about universal defamation laws in Australia by producing, and in the federal government's case revising, draft proposals to unify the various jurisdictions. In Queensland and Tasmania, for instance, potential plaintiffs could be defamed if they were injured in their trade or profession. The common example is publishing that a business has been closed down or offers inferior products. When made in other jurisdictions, such a statement would need an accompanying suggestion of incompetence or negligence to attract a defamation action, but the publisher should make sure he or she knows and checks that the publication is accurate, or risk an action for injurious falsehood. In any case, courts have looked at a person's professional reputation in a wider sense. In a 1996 defamation action involving two doctors, the judge said: 'In some cases, a person's reputation is, in a relevant sense, his whole life. The reputation of a clerk for financial honesty and of a solicitor for integrity are illustrations of this. The reputation of a doctor is, I think, of this character.'

Plaintiffs claiming defamation must establish in court that they were the subject of the publication. They might have been named or identified through other information or as part of a small group. A writer saying that all journalists were charlatans would cover such a wide group that it might be difficult for someone to identify themselves, but narrowing the statement to the Supreme Court pressroom, for example, would not only be untrue but would create the risk that an individual in that group could be identified and sue. Photographs can also create problems when the subjects are identified incorrectly, or those in the background are, by implication, joined with the subjects. Calling numerous men in a photograph 'a group of gangsters' might be problematic if the local vicar happened to find himself captured in the image. This is one reason, aside from a desire for accuracy, that photographers want to know the names of all the people in their pictures.

For the same reason, identification by name should be clear. Fricke (1984) examined a case fifty years earlier involving policemen who had the name Lee in common. An inquiry heard allegations from a long-serving prisoner that money had been paid to a First Constable Lee, of the Motor Registration Branch. A newspaper published an account of the inquiry, and two detectives, also with the surname Lee, sued successfully. Fricke also detailed defamation actions brought by married women after publications suggested that other women were either the fiancée or wife of their spouse. On one occasion, the husband gave the information to the photographer taking the picture. One further publication cost *The Age* newspaper $17 500 when it wrongly identified a man, not his son, as the person facing trial over a $56 000 robbery. Fricke, a County Court judge in Victoria, suggested the lesson was that great care should be taken in obtaining (correct) details when publishing. NSW Supreme Court judge Justice David Hunt said in a separate publication that most defamation actions arose out of factual errors by defendants. Most of them believed they had their facts right, but failed to check them adequately or relied on mistaken sources.

The dead cannot be defamed, although that position would change if the federal government's projected changes to defamation rules became law. But texts warn that an imputation against a dead person may reflect on the living. For example, suggesting that a businessman's crooked dealings had been part of a family operation which continued beyond his death might reflect on his children or spouse.

The extra proviso to prove defamation is that there is no legal defence available to those involved in the publication. Lawyers and journalists often have different perspectives on the situation. Litigants are not required to prove that a publication was false; instead, publishers must prove it was true. Journalists argue that this has a stifling effect on public debate because it places hurdles in the way of free speech and often benefits powerful or wealthy plaintiffs who can use the system to prevent criticism. Lawyers respond by saying that the media and others should not be encouraged to say things which are not true in order to damage reputations. They also say a careful reworking of publications by experts means that the position is not as difficult as the media make out. The reality is that publishers operate within a system that will be slow to change.

Legal writers have for decades called for defamation law reform, and many articles have been written from numerous perspectives. Publishers may use one, or a number, of the defences allowed, depending on the circumstances.

Justification

This defence is based on the truth of the published material. The argument is that defamation is designed to protect reputations. If a publication is true, a reputation is not lowered but brought to its proper level. The truth of a publication alone is a defence in four Australian jurisdictions: Victoria, South Australia, Western Australia and the Northern Territory. A publication must also be in the public interest to qualify for the defence in New South Wales, and for the public benefit in Queensland, Tasmania and the Australian Capital Territory. Truth must be proved to a court standard, in reference to each imputation found in the material, not just the words themselves. You might imagine that many pre-trial arguments are held in defamation actions to determine the scope of the meanings and the defences available. Courts will demand solid evidence, not hearsay statements in which you say what somebody else told you. Admissible evidence in court can include documents, photographs and tape-recordings, but the most common form is sworn evidence given by witnesses about what they saw or heard. They may be cross-examined by opposing counsel to test their evidence. It can be a difficult and stressful experience.

Courts have held that public interest is different from something which interests the public. In other words, public curiosity or interest in the latest gossip would not fit the bill. It must be something which might concern the ordinary reasonable person as a member of the public. Examples of public interest matters are the conduct of public servants, public proceedings of courts and other inquiries, the working of public institutions, and company prospectuses seeking investment from the public. Examination of a politician's private life may not be of public interest, even though it could arouse great curiosity, unless it had a direct and provable connection to that person's public duties.

The Fairfax media guide (Saddler 2002) puts the journalist's obligations under the justification defence in this way: 'Clearly, good journalism relies on accuracy and attention to detail. If in doubt about a word, always ask yourself "What imputation does this convey?" and "Can this be proved if it is necessary to do so?" If the answers are "no" then do not publish.'

Fair comment

As stated by Armstrong and colleagues (1995), if a matter is one of public interest, a commentator is free to express an opinion on it. The opinion can be extreme or unreasonable, but it must be held honestly. It must also be based on facts which are contained in the publication or are well known.

In defence of a defamation action, the relevant material must be clearly identifiable as opinion and not a statement of fact. For court reporters, this should be part of normal practice. Stories about daily proceedings are going to be written in a neutral fashion for a number of reasons. A judge is not going to be very happy if a reporter writes a running review of a trial as it proceeds, but a comment on the hearing at the conclusion would have to be based on the facts to have any credibility. According to the Fairfax guide, a statement that a restaurant's cutlery was grubby was found by a jury to be fact, not opinion. Likewise, the statement 'I believe the Minister is a crook' is capable of being taken as fact, not opinion, because it appears to be stating a fact despite the use of the words 'I believe'.

Qualified privilege

The fair and accurate report protected by qualified privilege must represent substantially what took place in court and also be free of malice. Armstrong and colleagues (1995) identify a defamation action against *Truth* newspaper, which reported on a case in which a man was acquitted of rape. The court held the report was not fair and accurate, despite correctly reproducing facts from the case. The relevant article dealt mainly with the woman's allegations and failed to mention significant parts of the man's defence. He was awarded $4500 damages.

A court report is expected to give its audience the same immediacy they would have if present at the hearing. As far as possible it must be an impartial account, correctly stating facts and providing balance between prosecution and defence. On some days the prosecution's allegations, or those of the plaintiff in a civil proceedings, will form the main part of the report. On those occasions, state the defence position and indicate at the end that the case is continuing. That shows members of the public not at the court that the report is not complete. Barristers can ask fairly sensational questions in examining a witness, but jurors are told that the evidence is the witness's reply, not the question. If a witness is asked whether he used a bomb to destroy a school filled with pupils and he answered, 'No', the evidence would be that he denied the allegation. The report should reflect that denial. In the same way, if a witness asserted she heard the accused boasting about his use of the bomb, then in cross-examination said she had made up the testimony, it would not be fair to report the first bit of evidence and ignore the second. It could be a better story anyway that a witness had made up the evidence, especially when the defence barrister tried to learn more about the circumstances through cross-examination.

This is fine in theory, but reporters will find cases in which it is difficult to retain an attitude of objectivity. At some trials, men will be accused of brutal attacks on children, or horrendous rapes and assaults. Particularly in the cases involving children, the evidence or general atmosphere can be very emotional. We heard evidence in one trial about a young child, whose body was subsequently found, apparently mouthing the word 'Help' as the car she was in stopped briefly at traffic lights. It was not difficult to empathise with the poor victim, but 'straight' reports of the case did not have to ignore her awful situation. If anything, a so-called sober account of the proceedings placed greater emphasis on what happened around the time of the girl's disappearance, rather than wasting words on emotive adjectives.

The qualified privilege applies to anything said in open court (though not in the absence of the jury while the trial is proceeding) and documents read as evidence in open court. Documents not so read must be used carefully. Damages of $2.5 million were awarded against the *Sydney Morning Herald*, which published parts of an affidavit suggesting a businessman threatened an opposing litigant with hitmen. The businessman denied the allegations and brought defamation proceedings. The judge in the initial case had read the affidavit in his chambers, but under Federal Court rules it was not regarded as having taken place in open court. According to the *Gazette of Law and Journalism*, an appeal was lodged against the decision, and the defamation action was settled on confidential terms.

Common law and statutory qualified privilege

The common law in States other than Queensland and Tasmania recognises situations such as making a report to police in which a citizen has a moral, social or legal duty to make a defamatory statement to someone else, who has a duty to receive it. A citizen who reported to authorities that his neighbour was setting fire to the town hall is likely to be publishing material that lowers the reputation of the supposed offender. Assuming the report was true, the citizen could be seen to have a public duty to prevent destruction of property and give information about an apparent crime. The communication must be for a proper purpose. Media interests have tried to establish the privilege for their communications but have failed in a number of cases. They are able to provide a forum for a person to respond to a public attack but lose the qualified privilege if the person launches a further attack.

Communication in political and government matters is given a qualified privilege in what is known as the Lange defence, named after an action in which the former New Zealand Prime Minister David Lange sued the ABC. The High Court said community members had an interest in receiving and disseminating information, opinions and arguments about government and political matters that affect the people of Australia but the actions of the publisher had to be reasonable. The Lange defence allows communication about a range of activities connected with government, but not the private behaviour of politicians unless it affects official conduct, or commercial speeches unless they have political content.

Publishers must establish that they behaved reasonably in communicating, and did not do so maliciously. Generally, to establish reasonable behaviour in publishing, they would have to show they

- had taken reasonable steps to verify the accuracy of the material
- had reasonable grounds for believing the material was true
- did not believe it to be untrue
- had sought a response from the person defamed and published the response.

Tight deadlines have not been taken as justification for publishing untrue defamatory statements, and the reasonableness of the publication cannot be evaluated in isolation from the gravity of the imputation. In other words, if you are going to say something you regard as important and serious, make sure you make all the checks.

In a defamation case brought after a column was published in the *Herald Sun* in December 2000, a number of defamation issues were debated. The Victorian Supreme Court awarded $246 500 damages to a magistrate who said she was defamed by the column. In 2003 the Court of Appeal dismissed an appeal against the verdict. By a majority, it rejected the Lange defence, saying newspaper criticism of a magistrate's performance was not a discussion of government or political matters of the type protected by implied political freedom. The column was an opinion piece, not a court report, said one of the appeal court judges, and the columnist had distorted the facts and given readers a false impression by leaving out some of the transcribed material from court on which he based his opinion. The publication was held not to be reasonable. The publishers failed in a bid to seek special leave to the High Court.

Before the appeal, media lawyer Peter Bartlett (2004) wrote an article outlining some of the issues in the case and giving general advice to journalists. He warned that judges not entirely sympathetic to the media would examine closely every aspect of preparation of a contentious article. They would also have the benefit of hindsight after publication, while publishers would have to show they acted reasonably, despite any mistakes. It is good advice. Not all judges are unsympathetic to the media, but prudent journalists should prepare as if they were. Courts are aware of the commercial nature and influence of media companies. They demand high standards when journalists assert they are acting in the public interest. As Lord Griffiths, from the Privy Council, said in one case:

> The media has enormous power both for good and ill, and it would be a sorry day if newspapers were encouraged to believe that under the shield of qualified privilege the reputations of individuals could be attacked by slip-shod journalism that would provide no defence of comment because the facts upon which the defence was based were not true. (*Austin v Mirror Newspapers*, 1986)

Protection from defamation actions exists in most jurisdictions when media outlets publish information after a request from the police or other official bodies. The protection extends to the material in the official request. Three States – New South Wales, Queensland and Tasmania – provide qualified privilege for reporting public meetings on public interest or public benefit grounds.

Consent

A publisher has a defence to a defamation action if consent is obtained by the subject of the publication, but consent must be made to the imputations or meanings of the words or pictures used. It would seem foolish to consider such a publication without comprehensive written permission.

Court reporters should see defamation laws as a good excuse to be thorough.

- Check and re-check notes. Make sure you have not mixed up the names of actors in court proceedings.
- Obtain as many identifying details about an accused, or parties in a civil case, as possible.
- Be careful with court documents, especially if they have not been read in open court. Check that fact, and be especially diligent if your source cannot establish the position.
- Be fair and balanced in your report. Do not leave out information because it makes the story look stronger. Within the time or space limits available to you, represent what happened in the court hearing.
- Never use a court proceeding as an excuse to pursue a vendetta, or to fail to report truthfully. Malice, if proved, would eliminate qualified privilege defences.
- Aim to exceed the requirement that your report be substantially accurate. Treating mistakes as the enemy will improve your story and your reputation.
- Take notes accurately and keep them, as they could be evidence in a future hearing. Also keep documents from the cases you cover. Potential litigants do not have to sue straight away – they have six years from the date of publication to launch proceedings.
- Report denials of sensational allegations and retractions of claims made in court.
- If your story stems from court proceedings and makes potentially defamatory statements, get a response from the person being defamed. You will support your defence and may receive more information.
- Assume you will need to convince an unsympathetic judge if your report is called into question.
- Check for suppression orders, especially if you have to leave court or cannot be there all day.
- In theory, it would be wonderful to cover every day of all cases in which you are interested. In practice, other commitments mean that is not possible. Cover the defence, check and report

the specifics which have been aired before the jury to give a correct impression. Include the defence in every story, even at conviction.

- Be wary of interviews outside court, press releases and spokespeople. These communications will not be privileged, and each will have an interest to push.
- If there is a problem with a story, do not take it upon yourself to apologise on behalf of your organisation. Make sure your supervisor and/or your lawyers know about it. A quick and well-drafted apology can help if you are being sued and facing a damages payout, but it requires skill and judgment.
- In a similar way, involve others at your media organisation if you have a story that appears risky. Calculating the risks of publication can be a subtle exercise.
- Understand the differences between criminal and civil cases. One newspaper was sued when it reported that a former senior public servant was facing charges over credit card use when he was involved in a civil case in which he denied liability for amounts charged to the card.
- Tell subeditors or the news desk if you see potential problems in a story. The embarrassment at being wrong about it is nothing compared with the potential consequences of appearing in court.

Chapter 5

Writing the (Newspaper) Story

Journalists are the link between the courts and the public. Take the word of a Supreme Court judge who dismissed an application by media interests for documents in a criminal case. The judge upheld a general right for journalists to have information from courts as long as it allowed fair and accurate reporting to take place. When reporters translate legalese into plain language for non-lawyers, fairness and accuracy should be at the front of their minds. As discussed in Chapter 3, journalists can publish normally defamatory or outrageous statements made in court provided the reports are fair and accurate. Added to the enjoyment is the pressure of deadlines. Court stories must be balanced, they must reflect the day's proceedings, they must contain basic details to establish their veracity and they must be written on time.

Basic details

Start with the attitude that you are the readers' eyes and ears. When you cover a case, you want them to know what the case is about. Telling them simple facts helps you to do that. It also helps later if you are asked to justify the accuracy of your report. And be accurate. The last thing you want to hear from a judge or lawyer criticising your story is: 'You couldn't even get my name right.'

A court report should contain:

• The full name, age, address (street name and suburb) and occupation of an accused in a criminal case. It is rare that a street number would be published in a court report, but it may be useful later if a photograph of a house needed to be taken later, or the resident interviewed. Be sure to get the number right. By identifying a person involved in court proceedings as fully as possible, you reduce the risk that someone with the same name will claim they were identified as the person before the court and therefore defamed. See below for examples. Check with prosecutors and court officials. Some defence counsel refuse to speak with the media; others will provide information in the interests of accuracy. In civil cases, the sensitivity of a claim may make it more difficult to obtain all the details. Try to make it clear you want to get the story right. Leave a note for subeditors at the top of your story if you have difficulties.

- Details of the charge. Copy the full charge and check if you do not understand it. In particular, be careful about the difference between murder and manslaughter. Include the date and place of the alleged offence.
- A record of the plea (i.e. guilty or not guilty) entered in criminal cases. At some stages, a plea might not be entered or might be reserved. Report that. In civil cases, outline the plaintiff's claim and the respondent's defence (i.e. in a negligence claim, until the defence case has begun, readers should know that a respondent has denied liability).
- The court in which the case is being heard.
- The name of the judicial officer hearing the case, and the names of counsel appearing in it. Check if they are a Queen's Counsel or Senior Counsel. In the past, it was common to include the names of instructing solicitors, but the practice appears to have faded.
- The correct names and details of witnesses. Some courts have made it a practice not to require a witness to declare his or her address in open court.
- The result of the hearing. It is simple when a jury returns a verdict, or a person is sentenced, but let readers know if the case is continuing or has been adjourned. If a judge or magistrate has made a specific date for the next hearing, include that information. Explain whether the accused in a criminal case has been granted bail or remanded in custody.
- The defence, if it has been made clear to the court. Check the progress of the case to make sure you do not miss defence evidence, or closing remarks by counsel if the defendant chooses

not to give evidence. Including the defence is part of a fair and accurate report. Even when a person has been convicted, it is still a good plan to mention a paragraph or two of his or her case.

A number of reasons exist for these practices. The first is to show your readers you made an effort to get the details right. Most of us should have read the surveys which rank journalists near the bottom when occupations are ranked for trustworthiness. Assume some readers will mistrust your motives and disbelieve everything you write. You can start building trust by correctly reporting the basic facts.

Another consideration is defamation. We have discussed the way captions and wrongly chosen photographs can be costly for newspapers, but reporters should also be sensitive about identifying parties to a court case. Remember, you are dealing with real people in difficult situations. It might be hard for John Smith to be accused of a serious offence, but it is worse for his namesake in a nearby street to be mistakenly identified as an alleged killer or rapist.

One colleague encountered an unlikely coincidence when reporting about a teacher charged with child sex offences. After the story was published, the reporter received a telephone call from another teacher, asking that a clarification appear in the paper to confirm he was not the person mentioned in the article. The teacher had the same first name, surname and age as the accused, lived in a neighbouring suburb, and had taught at some of the same schools, often being mistaken for the other man. According to the colleague, only the inclusion in the report of the alleged paedophile's (different) middle name and his exact address, with street name, saved the newspaper from a libel action.

A few years ago, another reporter had a separate near miss. An accused with a rather unusual name was charged with attempted murder over a 'road rage' confrontation. The journalist remembered the name as being that of the son of a convicted murderer. He also recalled evidence from the murder pre-sentence hearing about the effect of the killing (the father had evidently murdered his wife in brutal circumstances) on family members. Now, it appeared he had found news. The attempted murder accused had the same name, age and suburb address as the grieving son. Had he lost control while still affected by the death of his mother? The human interest is obvious. The family connection was not mentioned in a brief court hearing, but telephone calls to contacts seemed to support the reporter's conclusion.

Then he called police to check a couple of details. He did not have a middle name, street name, or date of birth for the accused. Sure enough, the details confirmed that he was a different person. He lived a few streets away from the son and was a similar age. Imagine you were the son who had lost his mother, then opened the newspaper to find you were wrongly accused of a crime, with the tragic family death blamed for the new offence. Do you think you might sue?

You might have found a unique angle, or exclusive interview. You might write beautifully. The story might be filed at a crucial stage of the case, for example a defendant in a murder trial giving sworn evidence that he did not commit the crime. None of this will matter if you miss a deadline. With exceptions for important events, television and radio news bulletins are usually broadcast at fixed times. Newspapers set deadlines for copy so their various editions can land at an interstate newsagency or over the back fence at the right time.

Filing on time starts during the day, while you are in court. You want to avoid having to leave a complicated trial at 4.15 p.m., with photographs to organise, news editors to call and two hours to read your notes, check details and write a story. Courts usually start at 9.30 a.m. to 10.30 a.m., adjourn at 1 p.m. for lunch (times can vary – in the Federal Court the lunchbreak can be 12.45 p.m.) and resume at 2.15 for another two hours. The best practice is to be on time, so you do not miss the submission of the day, made just as the case starts.

Many reporters think ahead. They underline interesting comments as they take notes, or use a marker pen at the lunch break. Others rule a line down their notebook and write short comments in the blank column alongside their notes when they hear a significant quote. I like to walk out of a session with an idea for a lead paragraph in my head. Almost two decades ago, a greatly respected colleague at our then afternoon newspaper could leave court, telephone a copy-taker (a typist who records the story read by a reporter over the telephone) and file a 25-paragraph story directly from his notes. Radio reporters must be able to write a few quick paragraphs and send their stories quickly if their case ends shortly before the hourly bulletin.

In the early 1980s, at another now-defunct afternoon newspaper, court reporters had a terrible choice. Lawyers make some of their best submissions close to the 1 p.m. lunch break, particularly in jury trials, because they want the important points fresh in the jurors' minds over the seventy-five minutes before court resumes. The same theory is used when counsel examine a key witness. Frequently, in court, the witness reaches an important stage in the evidence just as the clock ticks over to a scheduled break. This also means that a couple of 'refresher' questions can be asked when court resumes.

At the former afternoon daily, the deadline for the main edition was 1 p.m. Copy filed after that was reduced to a three- or four-paragraph brief at the back of the newspaper, if the story was deemed important enough. That meant the court reporter could spend all morning listening to pre-lunch evidence but had to leave up to fifteen minutes early to send the story by phone. If you were late, because the case was very interesting and you wanted to hear the definitive submission or question just before the break, you paid the price. The story did not appear. On some occasions (remember, this was before mobile phones), you could run to a nearby public telephone and beg for another five minutes from the news editor.

The experience of missing a deadline was a good teacher. The court staff at the paper learned to choose cases that were dealt with quickly. Sentences were passed earlier in the morning so they were more suitable for our deadlines, as were bail applications and summary cases in the Magistrates Court. Stories on trials and committal hearings were based on evidence given in the morning session, but reporters stayed for the afternoon in big trials in case their morning newspaper competitors missed an angle, and they could file the next morning for an early edition.

It is important to know deadline times and to communicate with the news desk if you are having troubles. Use the lunch break to look over your notes in a continuing case, or to make a start on a story that finished early. Reporters are slaves to the operation of the courts.

We have to be flexible. We cannot reschedule a hearing because the time does not suit us – the case will go on regardless. When waiting for a jury, it is good practice to have background paragraphs which describe the core issues of the case already written before you are called back into court. Jurors can deliberate for hours, days or weeks. Thy have a terrible habit of returning with a verdict late in the day when you are writing another story and have not prepared for their case.

Story length is another essential consideration. Court reporters should read their stories after publication. Are they changed or chopped in length regularly? Have subeditors frequently asked questions about the copy because they do not understand parts of it? Journalists should aim to have their stories published as written. When reading the published story, analyse whether most if not all of your copy makes the paper. If not, try subediting the story before it is sent to the subeditors, something not always possible because time will be short. But it is amazing how many mistakes are found, or sentences trimmed, because a reporter takes the time to self-edit. Look at the length of the stories published in the newspaper. If you are sending twenty-five paragraphs each time and they are cut to twelve, you are writing too much.

One former colleague said he stopped writing when he saw he was padding out the story with unnecessary detail. Also be aware that a newspaper's needs can change. A story may be slashed in length on a busy news day when other important issues are competing for space. On other days, news editors can call late to request two or three more paragraphs because the story did not quite fit the available space. Seek advice from a senior colleague if your work has repeatedly been substantially rewritten. Sometimes others can see things that are not apparent to the writer.

Writing the story begins long before you sit at the computer terminal at the end of the court hearing. Ask yourself why you have chosen to report this hearing instead of the others being conducted at the same time. One former court reporter called this process 'finding the sex angle'. What is it about the case that stands out? Why are we interested? Here are some of the starting points for court reporters in choosing cases to cover.

Celebrities

Some parties in court cases are already in the news. Politicians, sportspeople, actors, musicians are among those whose daily public performances fill media reports. Critics might accurately argue that media organisations prefer to report the information that celebrities want to keep from public knowledge. 'We built their careers and we can tear them down' is one version of a cynical cliché. If you accept the definition of news as something that somebody does not want you to write, it seems obvious that the celebrities facing court proceedings should expect publicity.

Unusual cases

Journalists seek novelty. Cases that provide a shock or surprise or something that has not been reported before are likely topics for court reports. Legal firsts, as long as the case is not too obscure for the perceived interests of readers, might make a story. Alternatively, familiar or 'classic' dramatic themes might increase the chances of a case being reported. A so-called love triangle, jealousy, a particularly violent or public crime are the sorts of themes seen as attracting readers. The killing of a well-off Melbourne couple described in reports as the 'Wales-King, or Society Murders' received widespread publicity, at least in part because it was sold as a glimpse into the lives of the city's normally private elite. Similarly, the killing of more than twenty criminals and their associates in an apparent underworld war and the separate prosecution of supposedly corrupt police were reported in detail by Victorian and national media outlets.

Topical cases

Court cases and news stories have two similar qualities. They are generally based on conflict and often deal with the personal consequences of a wider policy. Manslaughter and murder trials resulting from 'mercy' killings, when a relative or spouse is responsible for the death of an ailing loved one, demonstrate this point. Courts around Australia have dealt with damages claims related to asbestos-caused cancer. Policies about safety, mental health care, the duties of companies and government to provide reasonable care are tested in the courts. Through those cases, journalists can present concrete examples of problems, instead of relying on lobbyists, politicians and professionals to debate esoteric matters.

Comments by judges and lawyers

Judges, magistrates, coroners and other judicial officers sometimes comment publicly on issues, making a particular case newsworthy. The comments can lead to criticism of these officers, such as in a series of controversial statements made by judges in the past about rape. But they can also be observations about court security, prisons or the prevalence of a particular crime. Be ready for criticism when you report controversial comments by judges or magistrates. Try to explain their reasons for the comments, even, or especially, if they appear to be distant from community opinion. The worst aspect of current news reporting from the courts is a tendency to interview experts about controversial comments while reporting little of the comments or the context.

In 1994, appeal court judges in Victoria were criticised for their description of a case as a not very grave case of rape. The court's judgment explained the context of the remark. *The Age* reproduced some of this justification in a story I wrote which gave some idea of the basis for the majority decision. It did not stop one court officer from blasting me about the public furore that followed, but the report took information from the judges' publication, including their explanation of the phrase 'very grave case of rape'. You could imagine the court officer's horror if the report, which is reproduced below, contained just one mention of the phrase, and interviews with five lobbyists who were unhappy with the judicial use of language. Ironically, the case is a good illustration of the contention made later in this book that newspaper articles could contain links to legal websites, particularly in controversial cases. Readers could examine the detail of the decision and compare it with the short version in the newspaper.

Thursday 15th of September 1994 _ THE AGE (Late)
Pagenumber: 1 Section: News Subsection:

Rape was not 'very grave', say judges

Peter Gregory

An ex-policeman who admitted raping a woman in a car park before imprisoning her for two hours had his jail sentence reduced yesterday after the full Supreme Court found it was not a very grave case of rape.

Two judges said that while the case had one or two particularly unattractive features, such as the anal rape of the victim and the length of time she had to endure fear and humiliation, they hesitated to call it a very grave case.

James Smith, 30, formerly of Frankston-Dandenong Road, Carrum Downs, was sentenced in the County Court last year to 12 years' jail with a 10-year minimum after pleading guilty to two counts of rape, one of false imprisonment and one of recklessly or intentionally causing injury.

In a majority decision, Justice Crockett and Justice Teague upheld Smith's appeal against the sentence and reduced his jail term to 10 years with a minimum of seven-and-a-half years.

Justice John H. Phillips, the Chief Justice, said in a dissenting judgment that he would dismiss the appeal and that the sentencing judge, Judge Mullaly, was merciful in making the sentence for false imprisonment concurrent with the jail terms for the other offences.

He said it was uncontested that the woman suffered from a severe post-traumatic stress disorder with reduced sleep time and nightmares.

The court's ruling was made about 10 months after Justice Phillips and two other judges said the courts had to take an even more serious view of rape than they had in the past and foreshadowed tougher penalties to deter attacks against women.

In November, the full court said rape attacked the foundations of a civilised society. It said there had been increased awareness in the community about the prevalence of rape and the depth of suffering and permanent damage caused to victims, and such awareness had extended to the courts.

Justices Crockett and Teague said yesterday that almost all, if not all, rapes were grave cases because they were grave crimes, but they did not think Smith's case was among the worst rape cases.

There were many other cases that had characteristics allowing them to be called revolting, horrific, brutal, degrading, vicious or disgusting.

Those cases included rapes by multiple offenders, multiple rape offences and rapes occurring over several hours, often in a victim's home.

'There are other instances of the offence's perpetration taking place in scarcely credible circumstances of brutality and revulsion. On occasion violence with or without a weapon is used or its use threatened to secure the victim's submission. These are the cases that justify the description "very grave".'

Mr Justice Crockett and Mr Justice Teague said they were told Smith's sentence was the longest to be recorded for many years, and they doubted whether it would be considered fair. They said a sentencing Judge's requirement to heed public expectations had to be balanced against being seen to be giving way to public clamor for revenge.

The two judges said rape was a serious crime for which Parliament had fixed a 25-year maximum penalty that came into effect on 1 January 1992. But the usual reasoning that a maximum penalty reflected Parliament's opinion about the gravity of an offence might be qualified because a number of different maximum penalties had been fixed for rape in recent years.

If Smith had raped the woman 18 months earlier and there was no proof of aggravating circumstances, he might have faced a 10-year maximum penalty, they said. The maximum for the offence had increased one-and-a-half times in that period.

Justice Phillips said he was unpersuaded by submissions that the original sentence, equivalent to 18 years' jail with a 15-year minimum when remissions were allowed, was the sort of sentence imposed for murder. He said it was inappropriate to compare an effective sentence for four very grave crimes with a jail term for one count of murder.

He said later that the second rape added dreadfully to the woman's humiliation and degradation and that Smith's attack on the woman while imprisoning her was on a defenceless woman who had already suffered an ordeal.

He said Smith raped the 27-year-old woman vaginally and anally, then imprisoned her for two hours before she was freed by a passing motorist. At one stage, Smith threw the woman to the ground and punched her in the head when she tried to run to a nearby store. Smith said: 'Don't even think about it, don't be stupid.' Mr Justice Phillips said the woman was walking along a Frankston street early on 22 May last year when she refused an offer from Smith to walk her home. After following her, Smith grabbed her by the arm, dragged her into the car park of a doctor's surgery, then threw her on to a garden bed before jumping on her and raping her.

> Justice Phillips said Smith forced the woman into a freeway underpass and told her of his misfortunes. He left her when a motorist who stopped told him to leave. He said the woman had dirty, wet and torn clothing, many cuts and abrasions and dirt on her face and body.

If you are lucky, a court official or court media officer might learn of a planned comment, often made during sentencing remarks or reasons for judgment, and tell you in advance. Otherwise, be alert and be specific when you report the comments. Some judges speak carefully and indirectly about a topic. Be careful that in your reporting you have not turned a remark about a topic into something else altogether because you have thrown out all the qualifying words. Similarly, barristers can make spectacular-sounding submissions, but it is always wise to check the words in your notes when writing the story. Sometimes the 'sexy' quote was the only thing to liven up a dull morning in court, but when read back, it was nowhere near as interesting. Barristers can also be careful in the way they phrase their submissions. They play subtle games with words, but journalists have neither time nor space to reproduce them. In one case dealing with euthanasia, some reporters interpreted a barrister's remark as saying a particular course of action amounted to murder. Others disagreed, and a group spoke with the lawyer when court finished. She said that interpretation was not the case and explained the context of the submission. The danger for reporters is that a canny barrister can avoid controversy by softening or disputing the effect of an apparently controversial statement. Usually, if in doubt, I go back to my notes and make my judgment about what was said.

Sentences

Most readers would be familiar with stories in which a judge's sentencing of an offender is criticised. Sometimes a victim or lobbyist will make a general comment, such as that a killing or attack deserved more punishment for the perpetrator. You can understand the desire of a person affected by the crime to speak out. Courts also acknowledge victims of crime by taking victim impact statements, in which families and friends describe the effects on them of (usually) violent offences or corrupt conduct. Even if you include only one or two paragraphs of judicial remarks about rehabilitation prospects, remorse, previous convictions and personal background, it indicates at least that the judge had reasons for his or her decision. Others might debate the correctness of those reasons. Including them in the court story gives the public information about the case. I dislike reading stories which quote commentators and professionals about the correctness of decisions without including anything from the original judgment.

Events in court

More than a dozen years ago, reporters took notes during the sentencing of two convicted murderers, who received hefty sentences for a violent killing. Without warning, one of the men took a homemade weapon from his boots and slammed it into the dock. He and his colleague spat at female journalists when led by security officers past the press benches, apparently mistaking the women for another reporter who wrote an uncomplimentary article the previous week. Aside from the drama in the courtroom, security issues provided the story. How did the prisoner get the weapon into court, when everyone present was searched? What would the court do about it? Some of us were interviewed about the incident for the television news; others were quoted in the print reports. This sort of thing does not happen every day, but it illustrates the need to be alert. Understand the conflicts between the accused and victims' families; watch what happens and report what you see, not what you are guessing. Do not report that a witness cried unless you see it. Readers are relying on you to be their eyes and ears. They should not read fiction in your account.

Comments outside court

Depending on the statement and the speaker, interviews outside court can provide the lead paragraph for the most prominent court stories. Whether it is the influence of television's need for pictures or the copying of United States trends, post-hearing interviews have almost become the norm. Typically, the subjects are families of crime victims, but solicitors have become happier to put their clients' case outside the courtroom. Sometimes the court proceedings have not reached a stage in which the defence case is explained in full. On other occasions, broadcast reporters want a short summary from one of the parties so they can quickly explain their position in a court dispute. It is easy to use comments about a supposedly light sentence as a quick way to begin a story, but it is better to think about them first. What are you trying to tell the public? Is focusing on family grief the only way to write the lead? If you are quoting lawyers or company representatives, should you contact the opposing side for the sake of balance?

Some inexperienced interviewees might have difficulty expressing themselves, especially at a stressful time after sentence or verdict. Aside from the sensitivity in asking questions, reporters should examine their quotes for meaning. You do not need to change the words – in my view you should not – but a family member's remarks can be placed in context. A few of your words in parentheses or the positioning of the quotes in the story can explain the meaning of an apparently incomplete or obscure sentence. Beware also of the possibility of defamation.

Some interview subjects provide a comprehensive summary outside court of their theories about the case and the character of a convicted person or others. If you cannot otherwise establish the truth of these theories, it is better to leave them alone. Use grammatical devices or a few qualifying words to tell readers if you have shortened or joined quotes from an interview subject. It takes little effort to show that you have shortened a quotation to make it more readable. It is often necessary to do so when reporting judgments – some judges cannot express themselves in less than 60-word paragraphs.

Companies can release statements or comment outside court in an effort to better represent their position in a case. Remember, those comments do not attract the privilege that applies to submissions made before a judge or jury. But they can be used with care. In a hearing before a judge (no jury), the oil company Esso faced damaging publicity from a case in which it faced compensation claims over the 1998 explosion at its gas-processing plant at Longford, in country Victoria. Family members of a worker killed in the blast showed their anger when giving evidence about the company's failure to pay for the victim's headstone. Esso made no submissions in court but issued a statement outside the proceedings asserting that an offer to pay the $7000 remained open. A judge was hearing the case, so he could be presumed not to be influenced by the statement. As far as anyone could see, it was not defamatory. One reporter said he would not use the statement because the company had plenty of opportunities to make submissions in court. Another decided to publish, while making it clear that Esso did not make submissions before the judge. It is a delicate position, because big corporate entities have considerable resources to help them present their argument. The situation is different in jury trials – it would be unwise to think about including press releases from outside court in a report on a continuing jury trial.

Fair and accurate

As long as their reports are fair and accurate, court reporters have what is called a qualified privilege to reproduce the sometimes outrageous assertions made in the courtroom. Fairness should mean covering both (or all, in the case of multiple parties) sides of a legal dispute in a way that explains the substance of a case. Reporters covering jury trials usually write stories based on the opening addresses made in court by opposing barristers. A prosecuting counsel in a murder trial commonly outlines the circumstances of a person's death, outlines the legal concepts relevant to the case and explains why the prosecution says the accused person should be found guilty. In some States, defence counsel can then outline the issues or areas of contest in the trial. For instance, it might be clear that an accused was responsible for a victim's death, but the argument is whether the killing was murder or manslaughter. Even if the prosecutor produces thrilling prose and the defence sounds boring, you must include both in your report.

Some journalists make special efforts to ensure the 'boring defence bits' are kept in the published story. They will lead the story with the prosecution allegations, then include a paragraph or two of defence assertions, before returning to the case against the accused. The aim is to counter a common subediting practice of shortening an article by cutting out the bottom paragraphs (see Chapter 6).

Be fair by reporting the defence case if and when it is presented to court. Accused persons in criminal courts are not compelled to give sworn evidence, but their counsel will sometimes call on other evidence or open the defence case at the end of the prosecution evidence. If other commitments prevent you from attending court that day, make an effort to turn up when the barristers are summing up their cases. You can glean the essence of a defence from those submissions and, at worst, include those submissions in your story about the verdict. Even in the most awful cases, where someone has been found guilty of the worst crimes, the public should know they have presented a defence and be told what it is. Civil trials also feature addresses and the presentation of evidence by both sides. The same rules about balance apply.

It might not be possible to match every argument by a prosecutor or plaintiff's barrister with a reply by the defence, but you should report the answers to the broad claims made in court.

A fair report should not contain comment, particularly when a trial is proceeding. Publish observations, but be sure you are describing events visible to the jurors in open court. Do not refer to a 'shifty-looking' witness, or speculate that the defendant appeared to have bought a new suit and received a trendy haircut for the court proceedings. Try to be specific. Let the readers make their judgments from your words. For example, some journalists will say a witness has 'broken down' in the witness box if they hesitate for a couple of seconds when asked a difficult question. You will provide a better account by describing the hesitation. Did the witness wipe his or her eyes, bow the head, speak in a low voice? Did you actually see a tear?

Courts have been more concerned about substantial inaccuracies in court reports than about minor errors, but that is no excuse for sloppiness. Readers should expect that you will record accurately names and ages and other basic details. Double-check with the court and the lawyers if there are doubts. Ask to see dates of birth rather than relying on someone's memory that the victim was 'about 35'. Usually the details of charges are outlined in opening addresses, but check if you have any doubts. Charges can be expressed in convoluted legal language in court documents but can be shortened in a court report. A presentment, or document outlining criminal charges, might describe a kidnapping charge as 'detaining or enticing a person with intent to demand payment by way of ransom for the return or release of that person'. You can call the offence kidnapping, but be sure to describe where and when it happened.

The best way to ensure accuracy is to actually turn up at court. A few journalists have tried to build careers in going to one court, then leeching a story from compliant colleagues in another. The copy-gatherer writes both stories, looking like a champion to the unknowing news editor. This practice goes very well until mistakes are made. It is not a defence to a contempt of court allegation to say you were just doing what everyone else was. It is difficult when you are on the receiving end. Once, when I was filing a story over the phone to meet an early deadline, I saw a radio journalist rush into the room, take notes from my utterances, and leave again to file a story.

Frankly, I was too weak-willed to complain to his bosses, but he lost respect in that exchange. It was tempting to consider filing a few fictional paragraphs, then resuming the real story after asking the copy-taker to remove the false notes. But telling lies should not be part of your job. If other colleagues offer notes or describe sensational events in court, make sure you check through official sources. Seek transcript, check with lawyers, ask court spokespeople if it is a significant event. Think about the way you would defend your story in court. You do not want to say, 'I got that story from Harry. He's always right, so I could trust his copy.'

Length

Court stories can vary in length from three- or four-paragraph pieces known as 'briefs' to massive 50-paragraph efforts, depending on the perceived importance of the case. In one university assignment, I examined the length of court stories I had written over a year and compared them with those written by my predecessor at the Victorian Supreme Court. Newspapers might be more or less interested in court reports at different times. Journalists will write the same sorts of stories differently, or choose different topics, or perhaps receive a better 'run' in the paper because of their experience and reputation. Nevertheless, my study showed a reduction in the space given to court reports, from about twenty paragraphs to fifteen, over some twenty years. Allowing for the various factors that could affect the result, I assume that I might have fifteen paragraphs in which to summarise a day's court proceedings. Those fifteen paragraphs must still include all the basic details, a description of the events, at least one balancing defence paragraph, probably a paragraph or two of background to explain the case and one at the end of a continuing case to tell readers it has not finished. Given that a day's transcript from court can run to hundreds of pages and thousands of words, it is not surprising that lawyers and judges complain about a lack of context.

You cannot say everything in fifteen paragraphs. Don't try. One colleague counsels about being too clever in court stories. Remember that someone who has never heard about the case you are covering might be reading about it for the first time. Choose what you believe to be the newest or most important point, back it up with quotations or paraphrased copy, and balance it if you can with the other side. Read the story again before you send it for subediting. The best reporter can forget the name of the court, or a plea. Communicate with those working on your story if you see legal or factual difficulties. Tell them if you have written the article in a particular way for a reason. Remind them to publish the defence.

Usually, I include these in a note at the top of the story. You can say 'NOTE SUBS. Please include the defence barrister's submissions for the sake of balance' repeatedly over a year, but the day you forget, illness will strike the office and someone who has never subbed court stories will be working on yours.

Violence

Mercifully, journalists sitting in court have little direct connection with the violence described by lawyers and witnesses. Police photographs and videos of dead and injured victims are shown to jurors as part of the evidence in trials. Pathologists give detailed evidence about the state of a body, the perceived cause of death and the methods (often concerned with the maturity of maggots found in a decomposing body) used to estimate the time of death. Specific and sometimes upsetting evidence about the treatment of victims must be given in court to establish the facts of a criminal prosecution. In civil cases, plaintiffs are sometimes asked embarrassing and personal questions as they try to prove the effects of what they say is negligent conduct. In a room filled with strangers, they talk about their sexual dysfunction or basics of care that most would not like to discuss outside their families. Alleged rape victims will be asked specific questions about their conduct and that of their attacker.

Ask the many media critics and you will find a variety of views about the way you should report violence. Some argue journalists choose only the 'spectacular' cases and ignore the more common hearings concerned with domestic violence. Journalists are urged not to report the violence at all to avoid titillating or offending readers, or asked not to filter evidence so that a realistic picture is painted. It is the reality of life that media organisations are commercial enterprises selling information to a mass audience. Reporters will choose stories they think will interest their editors and present them as attractively as they can. Court reporters are no different, but they should recognise the seriousness of the courtroom. Usually editors are very sensitive about upsetting readers over the breakfast table. Talk to your news editor or chief of staff. Ask yourself if it is necessary for the story to include all the violence. On occasions it is needed. If a judge sends a convicted murderer to jail for life for what he or she describes as one of the worst cases ever seen, it is legitimate to tell the public about the crime. Glorifying the violence is a different matter. It takes no talent to find the goriest details and emphasise them.

Humour

Courts are serious places, but also sources of unintended humour. Courts hearing summary offences (those which do not go to trial but can be dealt with by a judicial officer) can yield funny stories.

One front-page story (complete with cartoon) resulted from an unfortunate judge's experience of being stuck in one of the court lifts. The building was undergoing work at the time, but it was hard to know exactly how the problem occurred. Clearly, his Honour was not happy, but the editing staff back at our newspaper were very impressed. The story appeared with a cartoon, in which a prisoner asks the judge: 'How long were you in for?' The irony of a judge being imprisoned, even for an hour, in the court lift, was too hard to resist.

Be careful, though, because there is a difference between recording something that is funny and making fun of someone. Humorous stories resulting from a court case must still be fair and accurate. Be careful during trials because judges and lawyers will be sensitive to the possible effects on juries of a story that pokes fun at one side or the other. Also be alert to making checks if you were not at court when something amusing was said to have happened. The public should rely on your eyes and ears, not those of other observers with their agendas and capacity to misinterpret.

Jargon

Every workplace has its language. Part of the problem in translating law to non-lawyers is coping with the use of Latin in the courtroom and simplifying complex submissions in an accurate way. Terms like *voir dire*, *nolle prosequi*, *certiorari* and *habeas corpus* might be common at court, but journalists assume quite correctly they are not part of everyday life. Buy a legal dictionary and check these expressions if you're not sure; occasionally ask others to look at your copy. If you spend long enough at the courts, you get used to the terms. Remember, most of your readers will not have been in a courtroom. Think of them also when you report complicated legal prose. Lawyers argue against the use of simple language because it does not reflect the subtlety of some submissions. Opponents can reinterpret phrases if they are not expressed in a precise (and usually wordy) fashion. Court stories would need to double in length to have any chance of making legal readers happy.

Shortening pages of submissions to three lines of copy must mean compromises. Read the text to be translated and compare it with your story. Have you made assumptions that cannot be substantiated? Some reporters, when confronted with an 80-page judgment, will either look at the summary sometimes provided by a judge, or concentrate on the first and last pages. The first ten pages usually explain an issue; the last five or ten set out the result. It is understandable when faced with an immediate radio deadline that journalists should get the basic details quickly and get them to air. But resist the temptation to ignore the sixty pages in the middle. Many gems are hidden within judgments – one judge who produced a judgment the size of a small book was once kind enough to hint at some of its legal highlights. The 'top and tail' read would have missed half the story. A good broadcast reporter could use one of the mid-judgment 'extras' as a lead for a story later in the day.

Getting a comment from a lawyer involved in a case can sometimes help the translation of legal terms. If a barrister or solicitor disputes your interpretation, explain the limited space you have to express the idea. Bear in mind that lawyers have their own agenda. They are representing clients. Their job does not include worrying about your task.

Structure

Some journalism educators favour a strict structure for court stories. Place the most important facts in the first two paragraphs, the plea and identifying details of accused or plaintiff in the third, followed by a paragraph or two of defence. Following text would explain the case and include a direct quote clarifying or supporting the lead paragraph. One of the early paragraphs would include the name of the court. If the case is continuing, the last paragraph would reflect that fact, and contain the name of the presiding judicial officer. The advantage for inexperienced reporters is the absence of telephone calls from exasperated subeditors trying to find out the basic details under deadline pressure. The last thing they need to see is a report with no plea, three different spellings of the accused's name, no mention of the court hearing the case and no charges.

English teachers sometimes suggest that every page of a novel should be relevant, otherwise it should not be in the book. The same applies to court stories. Read the story after you have written it. Are there 'padding pars' which add length but no extra meaning? Does the story flow? Are there unexplained terms or unattributed comments? Could someone reading the article for the first time understand what was happening in court? Read the published story as well. If defence submissions or basic details are being cut, tell the subeditors and change the structure for future articles. One experienced court reporter now makes a habit of including a 'defence' paragraph early in his stories to minimise the chances of it being cut from the end of the story. Another places the name of the judge in the early paragraphs for a similar reason.

Let your first paragraph introduce the important facts, but keep it short. Newspapers vary in their policies, but one former editor hated court stories with lead paragraphs of more than twenty-seven words. Copies of 45-word leads from sport and finance stories would be pinned to the noticeboard in the editorial office. Keep sentences short as the story progresses. If necessary, cut sentences in half and join them in a larger paragraph if they deal with the same idea or event.

Avoid mind-reading when describing the reaction of an accused or other newsworthy person in court. It might be accurate to report 'Mr Smith wept loudly when the judge announced his jail sentence'. It is merely a guess to say 'Mr Smith, obviously reflecting on the way he brutally stabbed his wife, wept loudly when the judge announced his jail sentence.'

In one episode of the *Frontline* television series about current affairs journalism, presenter Mike Moore is lecturing his colleagues about the stereotypes they rely on when finding stories for broadcast. He writes a number of them on a whiteboard – things like dole bludgers cheating on social security payments and other insulting terms that would only confirm audience prejudices. Later the executive producer sees the list and compliments Mike on it. He thinks Mike is finally getting the idea about commercial current affairs, and has produced a list of really great stories. The lesson for court reporters from this fictional example is not to get trapped by fixed ideas.

It would be easy to write a list of court stereotypes. You could find characters like grieving widows, violent men, emotional women, evil killers, devious thieves, and write your stories accordingly.

There would be no need to think. Just use the label and find the material from court that supports it. But you can write better stories if you look a little harder. You are caught to some extent in writing daily reports, especially from a trial, because you rely on the material provided by the lawyers and witnesses in court. But you might hear evidence that speaks about an offender's circumstances, or a victim's reaction to trauma, that helps readers understand better what has happened.

Chapter 6
Subediting and Photography

Subediting

Subediting a court story sounds easy. You have a space to fill on a newspaper page and a story to fit into it. You take out the bits that don't fit in the space, keep the essential elements like charges and names of the main players, compose a headline, check that all the spellings are correct, and move on to the next job. If only it were that simple.

Clashing egos, poor communication, false assumptions and risky guesses are some of the faults that can destroy the accuracy of the finished product. Reporters can be precious about changes to their copy, subeditors flippant or ignorant about the structure of the story. Arguments can occur about the paragraphs to be cut so that a story can fit the available space. Reporters like a remark quoted by Supreme Court judge Justice Bernard Teague (1998–99) in a legal magazine, and said to have come from a former *Age* editor: 'The strongest human drive is not that which pursues sex or food, but the uncontrollable urge to change another person's copy.'

Court reporters are not blameless, either. One newspaper veteran, who had a short subediting stint as he moved from courts to other areas, showed amazement as he described those of his colleagues who could not spell, write or compose an intelligible sentence.

Another subeditor told at one paper how some reporters were called 'The Untouchables'. The label meant that their stories were rarely changed because of their seniority and reputation for quality. Then there were those who considered themselves untouchables. They grumbled when stories were rewritten, made themselves unavailable when they were needed to check details and always insisted on the correct byline. One star would go out of his way to correct the copy of others and advise them on writing skills, apparently unaware that his stories were regularly rewritten and often reduced by half. Some subeditors would approach the 'pretend' untouchables' copy by making sure the story was in reasonable shape but not trying to improve it. They used the 'we've covered for this person long enough, let them hang themselves' theory to justify exposing the flaws in their colleagues' work.

Reporters often have another view. They are aware they have a qualified privilege (or permission) to report the sometimes defamatory statements or answers made in court provided they give a fair and accurate account. In practical terms that can mean making sure, over the course of a trial, that the arguments of prosecution and defendant, or plaintiff and respondent in a civil case, are presented in a balanced way. In a criminal trial, an accused might decide not to give evidence. That can limit media coverage to an acknowledgment of a not guilty plea and some details from an opening or closing address.

This is better than the instinct of some subeditors, who chop all mention of the defence case from a report because it is too long, or confuse the name of the accused with the police officer prosecuting the case. Others will change a factual detail in a story because they and their colleague at the next computer terminal are convinced the reporter has it wrong and do not make a telephone call to double-check. Below are suggestions – some provided by subeditors – to reduce the number of things that can go wrong. Out of a sense of balance, I will advocate some risk management measures reporters can take to help their workmates get it right.

Newspapers have used a variety of approaches to encourage accuracy. The *Herald Sun*, for example, employs a senior journalist to check court stories before they are sent for subediting, in an effort to weed out problems or ask questions of the reporter before sending it to the subs. Other, smaller publications assign a subeditor with formal or informal legal knowledge to deal with court copy. At one former workplace, another senior journalist and I were made responsible for the younger reporters and routinely checked their stories before they were sent. Whatever the mechanism, media organisations should make sure they avoid the 'sink or swim' approach.

One of the things judges like to hear when a journalist is prosecuted for contempt of court is that the media organisation has a system to ensure errors are not repeated. Why wait to go to court? Young court reporters should be trained, and helped if they make mistakes. Ideally, they should start on basic tasks like gathering adjournment dates or covering small hearings before being let loose on more complicated proceedings, but this is not always practical. Trainees can be thrown into many areas of newspaper reporting and can be asked to handle major stories. Senior journalists may be stuck in a long-running trial, leaving others to take on other cases. A small paper might have only one court reporter, and that job is left to the new staff member. The basic message is not to have an inexperienced person left to make mistakes that could be costly. Fight a contempt charge in court for a day or two, add up the costs for the lawyers and any fine that might result, then compare it with the price of training courses or good, regular legal advice.

Experienced journalists covering courts should practise 'defensive' reporting by anticipating the ways in which their stories could be misinterpreted or changed to make them wrong. Likewise, subeditors can use these simple methods to make sure court copy is fair, balanced and accurate.

Treat the stories as if they were your own

Almost the worst experience for court reporters is to open a newspaper and find their story has been changed and is now wrong. A paragraph might have been cut from the story, giving the reader the impression that Joe Bloggs the barrister, not his opponent John Smith, has made a particular submission. Mr Bloggs might be a senior counsel, but in the court story has become, miraculously, a solicitor from a law firm. Both of those changes have been made to my stories. Subeditors should remember that they maintain their anonymity, but the reporter's name is on the story. He or she must wear any criticism, often in the courtroom.

The fallout from mistakes can range from simple embarrassment to serious legal consequences. One newspaper editor raced down to the court after realising a story contained errors and was being criticised heavily by a prosecutor and a judge. He made a quick and unreserved apology, promised to fix the mistakes and saved his publication from prosecution for contempt.

Read the story

It is not as obvious as it sounds. Subeditors often ring reporters with queries about copy when they would have found the answer had they read another paragraph or two. Court reporters should not mind silly questions if the subeditor has doubts. In some respects, the sillier questions should be asked because it will mean misunderstandings are minimised. But read the story thoroughly, and re-read it after you have finished subbing it. One journalism educator says he insists that the job is only half-done without the second check. 'You've got to go back and read right through it again because you'll be amazed how many mistakes you can pick up (on the) second read(ing).'

Go back to basics

Ensure that all the main details are present. They include the names, ages, addresses and occupations of the accused, parties to a case or witnesses; the charges or causes of action; the names of judges, lawyers and the court, the plea in a criminal case, or the defence position (e.g. the hospital denies liability) in a civil matter. It is not pedantry. Coincidences, even incredible ones, do happen, and you can come unstuck in spectacular fashion if identifying details are missing. Remember the story in Chapter 5 of the teacher whose name led to his being mistaken for an accused paedophile. The inclusion in the report of the accused man's (different) middle name and his exact address saved the newspaper from the threat of a libel action.

Consult the source

Subeditors should remember that the reporter who wrote the story was the person on the spot who knows, or should know, the facts. A sub might be convinced that he or she has unearthed an error, or that a reporter has missed or buried an angle. It might appear that a paragraph might be expressed more simply or elegantly. But great care should be taken in changing copy without asking the author of the work. The reporter might have written the paragraph in a particular way to reflect the subtlety of a legal submission. Even a slight change might make the story wrong, or give a meaning that the reporter did not intend. If in doubt, check. And have doubts. It's no comfort that you and the person sitting next to you at the subs' desk were convinced you were right when you made that crucial change, only to find that both of you got it wrong.

Reporters should also ensure that they are contactable. Make sure the company has your home and mobile phone numbers, or write them in a note at the top of your story. Let the subeditors know if you're going to be unavailable. These sound like absolute basics, but it's amazing how often problems are caused when they are not followed. If a reporter cannot be found, it is up to the subeditors to decide whether any queries about the story mean there is a danger in running it. If the story is spiked, that's the reporter's problem. If you run it, and it's inaccurate, it's your problem too.

A call should be made to reporters when copy provided by news agencies is combined with their work. It's annoying enough for journalists to have someone else's efforts included in their reports. Presumably, if the details were important, they would have been used in the original story. It's worse if the stories are merged in a clumsy fashion or mistakes are found later. We should be clear in making this criticism. The vast majority of reporters working for news agencies write quickly and accurately under high pressure. But mistakes are possible. A check with the reporter whose copy is being altered by the inclusion should reduce the prospect of error.

Don't 'cut from the bottom'

One of the standard techniques of modern journalism is that a properly written news story arranges the facts in the order of impor-tance from top to bottom. But it does not always work that way in court stories. Reporters' talents vary. Sometimes the flow of the story means that a significant point appears lower than might have been expected. Cutting court stories from the bottom, that is, removing the later paragraphs to fit the story into the required space, does not work. Take the example of a report of the opening of a criminal trial. Typically, the prosecutor delivers an opening address outlining the charges and what are said to be the circumstances of the case. In some jurisdictions, the defence counsel are allowed to reply immediately afterwards to set out the points at issue. Cutting from the bottom might mean that the defence case is removed from the story, and the important balance needed for a fair and accurate report is lost. Read the whole story. Tighten loose copy. It's amazing how much space can be saved, leaving more room for the essentials.

Be careful with killers

Be careful about references to killers. A convicted killer might have been found guilty of murder or manslaughter. They are not interchangeable terms. Murder requires an intent to kill or do really serious injury, manslaughter does not. Also be wary about captions for photographs. In one case last year, a man was accused of murder, but his counsel asserted that he had committed manslaughter when he killed a work colleague. The caption under the photograph of the person killed described her as a murder victim, but that was the issue to be decided at trial. It was the jury's task to decide whether the offence was murder or manslaughter, not the newspaper's. This is the sort of presumption that leads to aborted trials and embarrassed media outlets. In the case mentioned here, the killer was convicted of manslaughter. Mercifully, neither the judge nor the lawyers noticed the caption error.

Headlines also require care. It can be tempting when a prosecutor says the accused committed murder out of jealousy to write 'Man killed for love' in the headline. But at this stage it is just an allegation, presumably denied by the defendant. You could write 'Man killed for love, court told'. The attribution can sound clumsy, especially when words are at a premium. There is no easy solution, it just takes some thought.

The rule to remember is that the court decides the facts, so do not pre-empt a judge or jury by writing a headline that takes an allegation as gospel truth.

Know the law

Family Court and Children's Court cases, and others involving children, can be danger areas. They can be subject to strict rules about publication. Ensure that identifying details prohibited by law do not slip through the net. Check the office stylebook or a media law guide. Don't be afraid to ask an apparently stupid question. Have doubts and raise them.

Pictures and minefields

Examine captions carefully and make checks if there is the slightest suspicion of any problem. An obvious example arises when the details in a caption differ from those in a story. It might be that ninety-nine times out of a hundred the story is correct, but it is wise to check. Spellings can be misheard; a reporter can have a mental block about a name or somehow spells it in the story in two different ways, only one of which matches the caption entry. Here are a couple of costly examples. A solicitor from a prominent legal family appeared before a disciplinary board and the case was reported. Nothing wrong there, but the picture dug from the files and published featured another member of the family, who was able to take legal action for a damaged reputation. In another case, a reporter writing a profile about a murderer sent a note to the subeditors explaining that there was a good sketch of the killer on file, but no photograph. Imagine his horror when he opened the newspaper the next day and saw a photograph of another man published next to his story. The photograph depicted a police officer. It was another expensive mistake.

Layouts and law

It is not a common problem, but the way a story is laid out on the newspaper page can have dangerous and unexpected consequences. A court reporting colleague was covering a murder trial in which one of the victims was a teenage girl. The story was fairly short, but the file picture of the girl was run prominently on the page over several columns. When they saw the report, the defence counsel and trial judge were outraged because they perceived the treatment of the story was capable of prejudicing the jury by arousing its sympathy. The trial was not aborted, but the reporter insists it was a near thing.

Similarly, another judge was angered by a large newspaper photograph and television pictures showing a man accused of murder being led to the court in handcuffs. Even though alleged murderers were generally known in the jurisdiction to be kept in custody pending trial, the judge was concerned that jurors would infer the accused had previous convictions. Again, the trial was allowed to continue, but with strict non-publication orders.

Know the background

Knowledge about a case, from reading previous stories, can help subeditors pick up reporters' errors. One colleague tells the story about a subeditor checking the report of a hearing in which a man was suing over an accident that left him with brain damage. Suspicion about names in the article – they did not match what had been published previously – led the sub to call the reporter who wrote it. Apparently she had copied some names from a previous story and had somehow scrambled them in her copy. A man identified as the defendant to the legal action was actually the plaintiff's best friend and one of his main witnesses. The check averted a possible libel action.

Beware of spell check and technology

The Age made two embarrassing errors when a mix-up in the use of a spell check program led to the surnames of a judge and a politician being recorded as 'dullard' not Gillard; the word 'Gillard' was replaced, not bypassed, during checks on the respective articles. The system has since been modified and other checks put in place, but it was not much fun for the newspaper having to explain what had happened.

Another difficulty can occur when a news editor, unhappy about the angle chosen by a reporter, makes changes to the copy submitted before sending it to the subeditors. The news editor sees version one, but sends on version two for further subediting. The second version may lack some information contained in the original work. It can cause confusion when reporters are asked about the copy. 'I'm confused about the way you've written the third par,' says the subeditor. 'I didn't write that, and I explained the problem a couple of pars later,' the reporter replies, referring to a copy of the original story. The key is for everyone in the process to suspend their egos. Change court copy only when necessary; avoid dogmatism and sarcasm when asking a reporter about a paragraph that does not appear to make sense. And keep a dictionary in the top drawer of the desk. It's more reliable and much more fun for those who love words than the computer's spell check.

Use of 'allege'

'Allege' is a code word used to tell readers that a case is alive, or undecided. For instance, an accused person at trial might be called 'an alleged bank robber'. If found guilty by a jury, he could be called a convicted robber, or if pleading guilty might be referred to in court copy as a confessed robber. Each of the terms indicates the accused person's status at different stages of the court process. Beware of tautology – there is no need to say someone was charged with allegedly murdering their neighbour. The accused person is charged with the offence.

Similarly 'Sergeant Plod said Mr Smith was allegedly murdered' or 'Mr Smith was allegedly murdered, the court heard' do not need the adverb. The statement that Mr Smith was murdered is the allegation.

Court reporters cannot shift all the blame. As I have mentioned, they can remain contactable after filing their stories so subeditors can sort out any difficulties with them. Here are a few more.

Read your story again

On a day with tight deadlines, this can be a hard thing to manage, but reporters should take a couple of minutes off after writing a story, then read it again. Mistakes can be spotted, confusing paragraphs clarified. When writing a longer story, it's easy to forget details or mix up spellings.

Consult the dictionary

When paraphrasing, check that the word you have chosen as a substitute for jargon fits the bill. Legal language is precise, if sometimes complex. Reporters might be translating legalese into English, but they should make every effort to make sure the translation is accurate.

Take your work home

Make a copy of your story. Take your notes and/or documents with you. It's much easier to answer a subeditor's questions with the relevant information in front of you than it is if you have to rely on your memory. If possible, read the story once more. You can feel like a goose if you have to ring the news desk to correct a mistake after submitting a story to the paper, but it's better than the feeling you have if it appears the next day and you have to correct it then.

Stay calm

Debates about stories are not always caring, sharing affairs. Sub-editors or news editors can be frank and blunt about their opinion of your work. If you have done something wrong, wear it. If not, and you want to defend your story, do so calmly. You won't get a result by shouting or insulting anyone. Back up your opinion with information. Both sides of the debate should be aiming at the same result, to have the best story possible for publication. If you still have concerns later, talk to your supervisor. In the end, the editor bears responsibility for editorial content, but the reporter should ensure the content is correct.

Read your story in the paper

The next day, especially if your story has been given a lot of space, see how it appears when published. Has it been changed much? Have you found any errors after subbing? Is there something you could have done differently? When you have answered the questions, get on with the day in front of you. Generally, court reporting runs on a daily cycle – you don't have too much time to dwell on the past.

Keep a scrapbook

It's a low-tech filing technique, but it is a simple way of keeping your stories together and can be helpful when a chief of staff is excited about an apparent legal first. More than once, claimed landmark cases have turned into something less thrilling after a reminder from the scrapbook.

Photography at court

Two women hug in the courtroom as their personal injury case is settled. Metres away, a newspaper photographer captures their emotion. He has been allowed to take pictures as the high-profile case ends. The next day, his work causes controversy as a competing media organisation asks why his shots were not available as 'pool' photographs.

A few hundred metres away, another photographer stands outside another court building. She cannot enter the premises to follow her target, but must wait, possibly for hours, until the proceedings have finished. Occasional text messages from the reporter inside court let her take a toilet break. She wears a hat and sunscreen in the autumn sun. Despite the chat with her colleagues from television and other papers, she cannot afford to relax. If the intended subject leaves the court – with or without a coat worn over the head – she may have only seconds to record the desired image.

Welcome to the contradictory world of taking photographs at court. Some courts allow photographers easy access to important cases if they receive a request in advance. Other circumstances demand patience, in sun, rain and hail, as the long wait takes place for a brief chance to find a dramatic photograph which complements a court report. As mentioned in the television section in Chapter 7, courts can offer limited visual opportunities. Sketch artists are regularly admitted to depict an accused person, or lawyers and judges, but photographers are rarely allowed within the court precinct. Access needs to be arranged with the judge's permission.

Civil cases dealing with money, often heard by a judge with no jury, are often easier venues for newspapers wanting to photograph inside court. Judges perceive that little emotion will be caught by the camera, and jurors who might have been distracted would not be present. Usually the pictures must be taken before the day's proceedings start so the photographer's presence does not interfere with the operation of the court.

At first blush, the prospect of taking an interesting shot from a complicated financial case would seem minimal. But the spectacle of a dozen or more barristers, with off-white wigs and black gowns, taken from behind and above, can present an impression of formality and uniformity that helps sell a story to a reader. On the other hand, less formal settings can provide an unusual image and a contrast from the customary perception of courts. Some years ago, a land claim made by the Yorta Yorta Aboriginal community was heard in an open tent by a river. One of the organisers seemed to think I was patronising her by my delight at the structure. In a clumsy way, I was trying to explain the contrast between sitting in a sterile, air-conditioned room in a city building, and enjoying the sounds of birds and the scenery interrupting my concentration as the argument turned to legal precedents.

Court anniversaries and other ceremonial occasions are mutually helpful for media organisations and judicial administrators. The news providers take some easy pictures which will also be useful as background shots to illustrate future stories involving particular judges. The event story is more likely to be run in the newspaper if an interesting photograph accompanies it. If the picture is suitable, it might be published later in newsletters or legal journals, after the photographer's permission is obtained. Some courts will allow pool shots to be taken at ceremonial occasions. This practice means that a selected photographer will be allowed in court, and the photographs (or film by television camera operators) shared by other media outlets. It also means the court reporter needs to be alert. Some organisations are better than others in letting their competitors know about pool arrangements. If in doubt, ask the court media officer or court officials if you see a photographer in court who does not belong to your employer.

Case-based photographs taken outside court require concentration, patience and determination. Photographers can begin recording images when the subject has stepped onto the footpath. It is a public place, and effectively members of the public are fair game. But once they are inside the building, picture-taking stops immediately, even if they are visible from the street through the window.

Covering court cases can be unpopular with photographers because the work is unpredictable. A hearing could be over in minutes or last for hours. Arrangements have to be made or other jobs redirected if proceedings develop unexpectedly. The results can be physically and mentally challenging. Many organisations now provide wet weather gear for the unfortunate 'snapper' trapped outside the court in winter. Waiting outside court can be like playing a game of cards. The photographers and camera operators from different media companies develop a rapport. They help each other to spot the location of the witness or family member they want to capture. But they are keen to protect 'exclusive' shots of court exhibits or family photographs organised by their journalist.

Even though photographers often have little time to set up their shots, and might be blocked by security officers and irate relatives, their work can illustrate the emotions provoked by court proceedings. Anger, relief, frustration, sorrow and occasional joy can shine from the faces of interested parties. One prisoner, wearing a buzz-cut hairstyle, grimaced at the camera, providing a tense, almost comical, appearance. Another defiantly raised his handcuffed wrists as he was led to a prison van.

Personal injury cases present different challenges. As photographers and television camera operators at court doorstops readjust their positions to get the best shot, they must show sensitivity. A young child who faces life in a wheelchair and has braved the legal process to seek compensation should not need to worry that he or she is facing the right way, and should not be frightened by camera lenses. Photographers should avoid the example of one professional and his driver who raced to one mass interview in the street outside the court precinct. The car screamed to a halt, the photographer jumped out of the car, fired off a number of shots, then leapt back into the vehicle, which took off into the traffic. The producers of the 1960s Batman series would have been impressed by the energy and sense of drama. Unfortunately, the victim was a little shaken by the experience. A representative of the law firm bringing the case let the newspaper know the approach was unsuitable and unnecessary.

Experienced operators see patience as paramount when wanting to take a court photograph. Hours of waiting can amount to nothing if a loss of concentration means the picture is missed. Access to prisoners in criminal cases can vary around the country. At some courts, photographers have a few seconds to capture the image as an accused person is led from building to prison van. At others, the transfer occurs behind closed doors. Most photographers try to give themselves the best chance by taking two cameras. One has a wide-angle lens, the other a medium telephoto lens.

Each has a flash attached. In some situations, a long telephoto lens is also packed. The 'laneway' shot at the Victorian Supreme Court is a good example of the difficulties faced by an awkward location. The prison van enters the narrow lane between two court buildings late in the day to collect accused persons held in custody. The laneway is dark, and photographers have only a few seconds to film their subject. They are standing in the street, behind the bars of locked security gates. Prison officers sometimes obscure their view, the accused move between light and shadow, and occasionally they bow or cover their heads in an effort to stay anonymous. News photographers generally use an automatic exposure setting in these circumstances because there is no time to adjust when the picture-taking begins. They must wait, prepare themselves, then stay calm when the action takes place.

'It's very easy to become excited and make simple mistakes,' said one photographer, a veteran who has taken court pictures for many years. '(You must) tell yourself this is a very easy picture to take. There's no need for any elaborate lighting set ups. It's point and shoot. The choice of lens (should already) be made, and (you should know) whether you need flash or not.'

Taking the photograph is only one part of the exercise. Identification of the subject is crucial. One photographer recorded two men moving between van and court, and asked security personnel if he had captured the accused he wanted. He had, but somehow a mix-up occurred and the wrong man was named in the caption attached to the picture. An accused who had just started a trial was mistaken for a man who had been found guilty of murder. It took a swift apology and correction to avoid a contempt prosecution.

The lesson is to maximise the chances of getting names right. Television camera operators regularly enter courtrooms – without camera gear – so they can identify the person they want to record. Television crews have advantages. They tend to drive from job to job, so they have storage space for their equipment, unlike the poor newspaper photographer who often runs up the road to the court loaded with camera equipment. Policies vary, but cameras generally are not carried past the front door of the court building. Once inside, the photographer should then make contact with the reporter and sort out the likely target. Don't be afraid to ask silly questions. A newspaper artist sent to sketch an accused one day sat in the courtroom and drew what appeared to be the right person, who was sitting in the dock with security officers on each side. The artist left, but the reporter received a telephone call from the chief of staff about an hour later, asking for a description of the accused. It was obvious to those accustomed to trials who the accused was and where he was sitting. But the artist could not identify the accused, he could not find the reporter and did not know who to ask until he returned to the office.

Lawyers in civil cases can be helpful, particularly if their client is pictured when a writ has been filed or a trial has opened. One reporter, even when such sources helped with identification, wrote the names out on paper and checked again to make sure the spelling was right and the subjects were named in the right order. If there are any doubts about identification, don't publish the photograph.

Minter Ellison, the law firm which advises the Fairfax newspapers in Australia, has prepared a photography guide outlining legal issues that arise from taking and publishing photographs. Some problems come from a lack of checking, others from poor communication. The examples suggest that great care should be taken with the use of file photographs (taken at a previous time and retained by a newspaper), which are used to illustrate a later story. Here are some suggestions from the guide, based on problems encountered at the courts.

Guilt of the accused

Even where identification is not an issue, nothing should be published that suggests guilt. A photograph of a person in handcuffs is probably safe, if nothing else in the headline, caption or article goes further to suggest guilt. If the photograph is taken at the scene of an apparent murder, with the person in handcuffs showing the police the scene, there is a clear suggestion of guilt. At the Silk-Miller police shootings trial in Victoria, the two accused men were not depicted in handcuffs until after the verdict. A judge hearing another murder trial banned pre-verdict publication of pictures of the accused in that case despite media submissions that the general public would be aware that most people charged with murder in the state were held in custody.

Attribution

Captions to photographs should correctly identify the subject of the photo by name and description. It is the photographer's duty to make sure the identification is accurate. Some publications insist court reporters check the identity of court subjects.

Contempt

To avoid impairing the impartiality of the court, photographs should not be taken of a judge or jury. As a matter of practical reality, courts frequently arrange for file photographs of judges to be sent to media outlets. In part this avoids the publication of old (and possibly unflattering) pictures of the judges when they were practising lawyers. Publishing photographs of an accused person could be seen as contempt of court. The justification is that the photos may seriously prejudice a trial because witnesses asked to identify an accused might do so on the basis of seeing a media image, rather than from their recollection.

The rule applies from the moment of arrest and, in certain circumstances, when arrest is imminent. The publisher and editor of *WHO Weekly* magazine were found guilty of contempt of court for publishing a photograph of Ivan Milat, later found guilty of murder, while his trial was pending. Identification was a crucial issue at trial, and the court held that even if the chance of serious prejudice was very low, any possibility that identification was an issue at trial would mean that publication of such a photograph was contempt. Even blanking out the face of an accused might not be sufficient if he or she was wearing a distinctive jumper when photographed that was also worn when the alleged offence was committed. The court looks at the time of publication. In effect, it asks if identification was an issue at that time in the proceedings.

Statutory restrictions

Statutory restrictions on taking and publishing photographs include:

- cases involving children: photographs cannot be published if they identify a child involved in the proceedings, any witnesses, or the venue of the Children's Court.

- sexual offences: any photo likely to identify the victim of a sexual offence is prohibited.
- Family Court cases: the publication of any photo that identifies a party, person related to or associated with or in any way concerned with the proceedings, or a witness in proceedings before the Family Court is prohibited.

In practice, there are exemptions to some of the prohibitions, but publishers must be sure they exist before using the photograph. For instance, the Family Court will allow publication of photos and identification of missing children for that limited purpose.

Chapter 7

Television and Radio

Television and the courts

It is a visual cliché, but the rolling media maul, with camera operators and technicians backing into traffic, seems to sum up the image of television at the courts. Television news needs pictures to present stories and courts traditionally provide few. Cameras are not usually allowed in courtrooms, although there are many examples of judges and lawyers being filmed at the start of hearings. Camera access is strictly controlled and usually does not extend to the filming of witnesses or an accused at a criminal trial. The flip side is that television reporters can have between 60 and 90 seconds to tell a story and must fill that time with pictures.

A long stand-up (the reporter stands or walks while reading part of the script for the story) outside court can help, as can an artist's sketch from inside the courtroom. But unless it is a short item to be presented by a newsreader, a television story from the courts cannot rely on words alone. The reporter who uses evidence from an interesting witness wants film of that person in her or his report. If courts do not allow the filming inside, television crews do it outside the court building, often in the strange procession of photographers and camera operators walking backwards up the street.

Covering courts for television means careful planning. The reporter must be organised before hearings are ready to start. Newspapers can have multiple journalists covering courts and radio reporters can cover a number of stories each day, with different versions of each, but competition from other stories and the limited time-frame means that the court reporter at a metropolitan television station will file one story per day, two at most. So he or she must pick the story of the day. If it fails to work out, or a competitor finds a better case, newsroom managers are not happy.

Television reporters (sometimes with researchers or radio colleagues) phone the various levels of courts to work out options for the day. They need to have their camera crews in place to record the arrival of an accused or plaintiffs at the desired hearing, then coordinate their efforts throughout the day. They are persuaders of potential interviewees, motivators and directors of camera operators and sound recorders, and checkers of the finished product back at the studio.

Finding the right story means lots of checking before court starts. A diary is essential. Newspaper stories are kept; adjournment dates mentioned in those articles are checked and recorded. Camera operators can be sent to brief preliminary hearings, even if it's unlikely that a story will result. Vision is recorded of the perceived main players in a case for use in later stories. File footage can be important at the end of a case, particularly if there is limited vision obtained from the latest hearing. Pictures from the original crime scene also add visual variety to a court report.

Dealing with magistrates' clerks and judges' associates can be a rewarding or a frustrating process. Some will have no idea about the sorts of cases that interest journalists. Many will distrust reporters, some with an almost institutional distrust, and will give them no more information than an invitation to attend court. The journalist's system of daily phone calls to contacts is hit and miss, but necessary. Court officials can be good contacts for reporters they trust and deal with regularly. This is where a reporter with a reputation for accuracy and sincerity can benefit.

Bureaucrats and other court workers are accustomed to the problems that a small slip or inaccuracy can cause them. Removing a staple from a court file is just about a hanging offence at some places. The reason? It might imply that someone has interfered with the file, changed the information, or put something in it without the knowledge of others involved in the case. Lawyers have been berated for using a red, not blue, pen on documents. If everyone else has to live with scrutiny and attention to detail, reporters might think this a good standard to emulate. Persistence, manners, and an ability to listen and ask thoughtful questions can be a great ally during daily checks.

Once a decision is made about the day's best story, the television reporter's next asset is the flexibility to change it almost immediately. Competition for ratings is high between television stations and their news services. Chiefs of staff are intolerant when another station, or a newspaper, gets a picture or story that you've missed.

'They are happy when you do (have an exclusive) and congratulate you. And you feel like you have to explain yourself when you don't have it,' said one reporter. And a former colleague added: 'At the commercials (stations) you are more likely to have to explain yourself the next morning. It depends how experienced you are and . . . if the boss likes you. They'll take your word and know that you really did try your hardest, but if the boss is in a bad mood, or doesn't like you, then they can really rip through you.'

Television reporters spend much of the period before a hearing starts outside the courthouse, directing their camera crews about the right targets to film as they approach the building. The process continues inside the courtroom. Reporters bring camera operators to the media benches and point out the witnesses and relatives whose images they want.

While crews patrol outside at the 75-minute lunch break, reporters use marker pens to sort out the best lines for their stories. During the morning's proceedings, they have discreetly answered a number of text messages from their producers, or chiefs of staff. Courts usually insist on mobile phones being switched off during hearings, but television journalists often leave them on the silent ring mode. Even experienced court reporters can find themselves switched across a city to another (non-court) story at short notice.

Convention says the 'stand-up' is shot outside court, complete with traffic noise. Unless the story is a major one, most television journalists drift away from the courts at about 3.30 p.m. That allows them enough time to return to the television studio and marry their script to the vision selected by an editor.

Experienced reporters can direct the editors about the footage they want for their stories, but senior editors can be sensitive about being told the obvious. 'The journalist should always check the finished copy before it goes to air . . . because it's the responsibility of the journalist that the right pictures are put with the (correctly identified) person,' one senior reporter said. A colleague said she often gravitated towards working with one editor who had an instinct for identifying legal dangers despite a lack of formal training.

If television has changed court reporting, its effects are felt most in the impromptu press conferences or 'doorstops' held after important hearings. The interviews, with family members of murder victims, or plaintiffs in personal injury cases, provide the emotion and pictures that television stories demand. Rosters are organised between journalists to ask family representatives if they will talk on camera. It's a sensitive request. The sister of one murder victim said after a sentence was passed that the court proceedings brought back the pain and sense of loss that she presumably had tried to control in the years after her sibling's death. Smart reporters will not try to push demands for an interview. Aside from the sensitivity of the situation and consideration for victims and families, it serves little purpose to have the subject of a press conference offside.

All reporters should appreciate the brief but emotional relationship they can have with those affected by a crime or long-running case. One convicted murderer successfully appealed his finding of guilt and won a new trial. The fathers of his victims became the family spokesmen. As he travelled through the legal system again, they were available for comment at the new (guilty) verdict and after sentence. Again he appealed, but this time failed. If memory serves, he attempted to take his case to the High Court, but lost again. The process was over. We asked the victims' fathers for one more comment and they obliged. Then one turned to us and shook our hands. 'I hope you don't mind me saying this, but we would be happy if we never saw you again.' He was not being rude. Every time he saw the court reporters he was reminded of the sadness and violence of his child's passing.

One senior television reporter advocates honesty in approaching victims. 'I reckon the secret is to be honest and not to try and really spin a line. Most of the time people are just pointing at you and going "You're the media" and they hate you until you go over and say "This is my name and this is why we are here." And you just explain what it is and it would be helpful for the story and are you interested in speaking with us? But it's really hard and it doesn't get easier, because you're dealing with people whose . . . lives are shattered and it's such a big thing in their lives. Some people surprise you and say "Well, yeah, we'd really like to speak" and some people just tell you where to go. It's awful having to ask, especially if you have to ask the family of a dead baby, "Do you have a photo?" I mean, there's no easy way to say that.'

Journalists have a number of lines they use to persuade the families to respond. Some speak about tributes, others suggest they want to make sure such tragedies can never recur. The latter approach is hated by some but justified by others, especially after a coronial hearing over the death of a young child because of faulty bedding or other equipment. The worst attitude is to treat the interview like a game – look very concerned for the cameras, ask all the right questions, then begin cynical jokes the moment the family walks away. Mercifully, few court regulars react in that way.

Television dominates the post-court press conference. Interview subjects are asked to walk to a clear space where they can easily be filmed. Questions begin after the crews are ready with cameras. Reporters stand towards the front of the media scrum and ask questions so the interviewee is looking towards the lens. The worst result is having an inconsiderate newspaper hack standing to the side of the conference and having the subject turn his or her head aside to answer. A similar question might be asked again to get the same answer while the family member is facing the camera.

Competition between stations can cause paranoia among reporters. Phone calls are made and theories advanced if a rival and crew are not present at what seems to be the day's best story. One technique is to keep moving around the courts on a quiet day. At one press conference, a commercial television journalist obviously spotted an interview in the street from 100 metres away. He had not attended the case, but saw competitors present. Recognising the interviewee, he marched up at the end, introduced himself and asked what the case was about. By asking simple questions, he obtained a simple quote that the more knowledgeable and involved questioning from others failed to elicit.

Critics point to clichéd questions put by the broadcast media, but the most obvious query sometimes gets the best answer. 'How do you feel?' is often used, though derided by many. But it is one of the questions victims do not get asked publicly in court. Victim impact statements are now part of court proceedings. They are available to judges, though not usually to journalists, to show the effects a crime can have on victims or their families. In a more complicated fashion, they are the judicial equivalent of 'How do you feel?'

Here is the advice one young reporter received when she was writing court stories for television – keep it short, keep it snappy, no legal jargon. The time allowed to tell your story flies past. Television reporters cannot waste words. Their audience might see their news item only once. Complicated or confusing language is assumed to distract. Viewers do not have the luxury of reviewing the report, unless they are diligent or obsessed enough to video-tape news bulletins. Some newspapers are happy to use legal terms like *pro bono* (lawyers providing services for free) or *nolle prosequi* (a non-prosecution which can be reactivated with fresh evidence), but television prefers a simpler message.

The most colourful quotes from a lawyer or judges can be emphasised on screen through graphics. The words appear on screen as the newsreader presents the news story. Reporters have mixed feelings about graphics. In some cases they can lead to too much writing and take away from the pictures which are supposed to be telling the tale. The journalist can use a stand-up to present the most significant comments made by a judge in sentencing. Pictures from the case can be found to illustrate the words.

One technique has an artist sketching scenes from a re-enactment of a crime. The sketches are presented on screen one after the other in quick succession, almost like a slowed-down cartoon. In the 2002–03 Silk-Miller police shootings trial in Victoria, the images appeared to put one station's audience at the scene of the double murder.

Another way to bring viewers into a story is to describe the drama of courts. Clashes between opposing sides, the emotion of families and friends of a crime victim can add to the audience's sense of being part of the proceedings. If journalists are the public's eyes and ears, they should describe what they see and hear.

A word of warning. Be sure to stick to description rather than interpetation, especially when a jury is hearing the case. Judges assume that jurors, as members of the public, can be influenced by media reports. Presenting an opinion about events in court or posing a clever question at the end of a report has caused problems in the past.

Radio and the courts

It's a cold day at the court as media representatives wait for the accused sex offender to be released on bail. The television journalists want pictures; the newspaper reporters curse early Friday deadlines. It's just after noon, and their radio colleagues have already filed four stories about the case. By mid-afternoon they will have written more. The paperwork for the accused is taking time, the court has numerous exits and the radio reporters are trying to sketch out stories on their notepads while trying not to miss any potential interviews. They need to record all the sound their television competitors capture and get it to air first. Pressure is heightened when a hearing finishes close to the hour. Do you file a story and miss the interview, or vice-versa? The daily deadlines of other court reporters are compacted into hourly cycles. Radio reporters are often those most on edge at the courts.

Radio journalism is often described as personal and immediate communication. One former reporter and producer says radio is 'right now'. Stories are changed and updated throughout the day in radio news bulletins. Court reporters must juggle their commitments. They have to leave court in time to file stories that will meet hourly bulletins, fit in interviews with program hosts from their stations and organise themselves to avoid missing important interviews outside court.

They must write tightly. They have forty-five to sixty seconds at most to tell their stories. According to one reporter, the standard reading speed for radio is three words per second; that allows 180 words in a minute-long report, 135 words if the reporter has forty-five seconds. In print terms, that means four to six paragraphs. Within those limits, the journalist includes the essential elements of identifying the accused or parties in a civil case, mentioning the charges or issues being tested, and maintains balance by stating a defence. The report might feature a short 'grab' from an interview given outside the courtroom. It must be written at speed and filed before the hour, to let subeditors check it before a bulletin. One young veteran of radio and newspapers compares writing radio stories with grabbing a large quilt and trying to stuff it into a pillow case.

The key is preparation. Radio reporters start work well before court begins. The size of most newsrooms means that those metropolitan journalists lucky enough to have a court round must report from every jurisdiction in their city. Newspaper journalists might be assigned to different levels of court or have a pool of reporters to cover the different cases being heard each day. Radio court reporters must choose and gamble.

They rely on court clerks, judges' associates and media officers to be available and willing to tell them about the names on their court lists. After collecting the information, they work out their priorities. Sentencing hearings, for example, can be high on the priority list. The radio journalist can hear a judge summarise a case, deliver a penalty, and possibly make comments on a public issue in time to send a story for the 11 a.m. bulletin. Most court cases start at 9.30 a.m. or later, making it difficult at times to send stories before 11 a.m. Radio ratings are perceived to drop off after 5 p.m., leaving court reporters a limited number of daytime bulletins as the target for their story-telling. The exception might be a prominent case in which an important hearing is scheduled for the next day. Preview stories are filed the night before the hearing, to be used in early morning bulletins. The items are updated when the case resumes or is finalised.

Filing for radio requires a quickly written report which is filed to the office by phone, an ISDN line at a remote pressroom, or recording and editing back at the main newsroom. For court reporters, that usually means leaving a hearing ten to twenty minutes before the hour. Radio reporters can miss details because they are out of court, but they must take the risk so their report can be aired. Many will have some background paragraphs written beforehand, so they can add a news angle to the top of the story. According to one reporter, that process can be repeated each hour when covering an important case.

'If you're doing a running court case, what you're doing all day, for each hour, is freshening up the lead (paragraph). The rest of it, somewhere in the base of the story, is the core (of the report) . . . You've got seven goes at the same story. You've got to assume the audience is hearing it for the first time.'

The hardest story to write on a busy day can be the first. Radio reporters need all the necessary details beforehand, because they might need to rush out to file while the court proceedings are continuing. Newspaper journalists, in particular, have the luxury of waiting. At a break, they can check spellings, names and charges, and other identifying details. Some radio journalists carry newspaper clippings of previous stories about the case. If they are careful, they will have checked with barristers or court officials that the clippings are correct. A commercial radio reporter said the day's first story is where the biggest dangers and pitfalls lie.

'Because you don't always have all the information, you've got your office breathing down your neck, saying "We want it, we want it, we want it." Then you've got program crosses (interviews with radio announcers or commentators) to (deal) with. Sometimes it's interstate crosses, sometimes you're doing crosses with TV networks . . . and in the meantime you're missing stuff that's in court.'

One shortcut is to have pre-written stories already stored in the newsroom's computer system. A jury returns with its verdict in a big murder trial at five minutes to the hour. Short of filing live, with no notes or preparation, there is no time to write the required six paragraphs.

'You do a guilty verdict (story) and a not guilty verdict (story) and (they're) back in the system at work. All it takes is one phone call to go, say, "Guilty" and they run the story that says this person has just been found guilty,' says the commercial reporter.

The flaw is a misheard instruction over the telephone, or the use of the wrong story back at the radio newsroom. In a tense and rushed atmosphere, with little time before the bulletin goes to air, it is easy to make a mistake. It takes little insight to work out that only experienced and practised reporters should rely on pre-written copy.

One ABC reporter said she would bash out the basic details for a story if close to deadline – name, age and suburb of an accused, plea, court, result – then look again at her notes before the pressure resumed. Using a highlighter pen, she would pick out the quotes or issues she wanted to report for the rest of the day. This practice was most useful when a court decision was delivered early in the day, or a hearing finished sooner than expected. Otherwise, she would need to return to court. When the issues were identified, the journalist would tick them off as she used them in multiple stories during the day.

After typing everything she wanted to say, she would then check the story to see if it fitted the time limits generally imposed. The pressroom computer automatically updated the story length, so it was a simple matter to adjust the script. Typically, a direct quotation would be paraphrased, a whole issue eliminated and used the next hour, and sentences cut to reduce the number of words.

When audio facilities were available, the reporter would record one or two voice reports so the whole story was told at least once, then mix those reports, quotes or 'grabs' from interviews and other paragraphs in stories as the day developed. An editor dealing with one high-profile case rang to say that listeners had to wait two or three sentences before they heard new evidence in the journalist's reports. 'So I had to come up with ways to launch straight into evidence and just drop the essentials – name and charge and the fact that it was a committal – elsewhere in the body of the story.'

The reporter also checked a few times each day to make sure she was giving subeditors the sorts of stories they wanted. If many stories from other journalists were filling bulletins, they may only want a few paragraphs and a grab, instead of a full voice report.

Compounding the problem is the building of the radio bulletin. A five or ten-minute bulletin might have staples like sport and weather together with some reworked or 'freshened' copy. But a lot of work can be done in the last five minutes. National and international stories are mixed with local items. Reporters can file late, hoping to beat the hourly deadline with information they have just received. A late-breaking political story or terror attack or city siege can upset the running order. In that atmosphere, subeditors might miss a mistake or ambiguity, especially from a trusted reporter.

A story might be filed from a rape case, for example, in which a husband was accused of sexual offences against his wife. Mentioning the husband's name might identify his wife, which would breach laws preventing the naming of alleged sexual assault victims. If the reporter slips up, and the detail is missed during production, the station can be in trouble.

Technology changes in radio, but the basic needs remain: information from a reporter and the voice of an interview subject. One of the best interviews I have heard was held early one evening after an older man suffering a debilitating disease won a personal injury claim against his former employer. An ABC radio journalist interviewed him minutes after the victory. He explained that the disease meant his life was over but that he could now provide for his family. The journalist asked few questions. She let the man show his dignity and sincerity as he quietly explained his situation. The story probably ran on one or two bulletins that night, then faded from the airwaves as the overnight reports were received. It was a stunning example of letting the interviewee tell his story. What a pity many listeners missed the chance to hear it.

The daily reality is different. Television demand for visual images has turned informal conversations with those affected by cases into a regular ritual outside court buildings. A group of camera operators, technicians, photographers and radio journalists wait outside for victims, families or lawyers to emerge, while other reporters take turns inside to approach their potential interviewees. The broadcast media have similar aims in seeking interviews. The reactions to legal decisions update the stories beyond the formal process in court. They also provide emotion, ranging from anger at sentences passed, to sadness, and sometimes a mixture of hatred and sympathy for an accused. While television can take both sound and vision from the mini press conferences, radio must have clear audio reproduction.

It can seem insensitive to have microphones pressed near a grieving relative, but conditions outside court, usually near the centre of a capital city, are far from ideal. Aside from the normal traffic noise, some car and truck drivers appear to think it is tremendously witty to sound their horns just as an interview subject explains a perceived injustice. Manners are also required as camera operators want uncluttered vision of those speaking, while radio employees desire to be as close as possible with their microphones to gain sound that is reproducible when used with a report.

Print and radio reporters see the mini press conferences conducted outside court as television-driven, with a 'herd instinct' demanding predictable answers from clichéd questions. According to one ex-ABC staffer: 'It's almost mandatory now, where you get a statement along the lines of "He's got five years, we've got a life sentence," that sort of phraseology. The TVs are quite happy with that, they'll make do with that, but the pressure is on radio to make sure that they not only get it, but they get it on air before the television gets it on air to show that they're on the spot as well.'

Another radio colleague sees a cynical motive to produce tears when family members are asked to describe the sort of person their dead relative – killed in a car crash or in tragic circumstances by their former partner – had been. 'I reckon it's a really ordinary thing, because ... rarely do you see that grab run. And I can't work out why they ask that, other than to get tears. I think that's very, very ordinary to torment people's emotions like that, when they are feeling particularly fragile ... and that's a question I certainly don't ask.'

Program crosses are usually short conversations between reporter and announcer. They are perceived to convey a sense of immediacy to listeners and an image that the reporter is on the spot, waiting to provide the latest information. The chatty format can yield impressions or conversations that cannot be placed in a news story. Reporters believe they can lack control in the segments, especially when dealing with an announcer unused to courts or indifferent to issues like contempt of court or defamation. It might be unlikely that jurors considering their verdict are listening to the drive program on the ABC, but it is worth being cautious when the announcer asks 'Well, is he guilty?' or 'When do you think the jury will come back?' One journalist was asked, on air, the former question on the first day of a jury trial. An unwise answer might lead to lawyers asking for the trial to be aborted, because jurors could potentially receive public information from outside the court proceedings encouraging them to take a particular course of action.

The wary journalist, in her second or third year on the road, used a tip from a more senior colleague: 'Somebody had said to me somewhere along the line, "If they say that to you, you say, that's what the jury will decide." And I just gave (that answer), even though it sounded a bit rude. I thought, you idiot.'

Many radio reporters have felt foolish by forgetting spare mini discs or cassettes, or having batteries run out during an interview. The problem is exacerbated at court. Most interview prospects are tense, if not unwilling. They have possibly been asked to wait outside the court building while camera crews assemble and prepare themselves. After unburdening themselves about an incredibly stressful experience, they should not be expected to hear a cheery 'Sorry, my battery ran out. Can we do it again?' Professional, as well as humane, considerations also support efficient preparation.

The first grab is always the best. One former radio colleague used to infuriate television reporters by sneaking a quick interview with grieving families, then racing off to file while the rest of the broadcast media tried to prepare themselves for another effort. Almost invariably, they would complain that the radio fellow had taken the best lines. It sounds fine in a competitive industry, but the families were the ones facing a second interrogation as everyone else tried to catch up.

Radio equipment – known colloquially as the 'kit' – should be treated like the newspaper reporter's pens and notebook. Make sure the mini disc or cassette works and fits the player. It is embarrassing to turn up to a story, about to record, and find lights flashing on the player to indicate 'no disc'. It is not as simple as borrowing a pen. Reporters have been known to beg favours (and audio) from their competitors or sadly tell their supervisors about technical problems that seem to have ruined their interview.

It seems very basic, but the sound, not the script, is vital for radio court reports. Producers preparing bulletins hate running the same voices, and same stories, all day. Numerous grabs can be taken from one interview and used in a variety of stories from a big case. Disaster can appear to be the norm. Stories are legion about journalists who think they have recorded the most poignant comments, only to be disappointed when they return to their studio. You have your recorder, the tape is in, the batteries work, and there's a scrum of journalists pressing around, when someone inadvertently pulls out the microphone lead.

Audio tape-recorders are sometimes favoured because it is easier to control the sound levels, but they come with a price. The old ABC-issue recorders produced high-quality sound but are heavier than mini disc recorders and take longer to rewind and find the desired interview segment. Microphones are obviously essential, but microphone stands (a flat surface useful during a longer interview or press conference) can be rare. One reporter confessed to swiping a stand from the office, while another from a different employer said somebody stole her stand. She confessed to using her wallet as a microphone stand, a dangerous practice just after payday.

The development of the internet has changed radio journalists' appreciation of the written word. They were always conscious of finding the correct pronunciation of individuals' or placenames, but the use of news stories on radio websites means spelling is much more of an issue.

Producers usually speak with the journalists before the interviews, but that does not prevent surprises, as three radio reporters discuss below.

> *Reporter 1:* Sometimes they do ask you questions and you just have no idea. It's an issue you didn't even think of. It does happen. If you ever hear a radio journalist say 'Yeah, that's a question they do have to answer', or 'Yeah, we're actually trying to find that out. As soon as we get that info, we'll get back to you . . .'
>
> *Reporter 2:* That's not quite clear at the moment, but what I can tell you is . . .
>
> *Reporter 3:* You often hear the journalist go off on another tangent, and you'll pull something out . . . something else that's good that they haven't mentioned. You can't answer that question, so you go, 'Well, that's not clear (but) one thing I can tell you . . .'
>
> *Reporter 2:* You've just got to get yourself back in control.

Many crosses are made to local programs, but interstate and international producers can request interviews on big stories. ABC reporters can be asked to speak with multiple interstate programs broadcast in different time zones, as well stations in New Zealand, the United Kingdom and the United States. The trick is time management. A reporter might be asked to tell the same story eight different times, with a five- or ten-minute wait each time before the (live, not recorded) interview can start. Undertaking four crosses in an hour could mean an absence from court of between fifteen and forty minutes. It can be necessary to say 'No'. One school of thought says the priority is news. But news directors feeling proud because their staff member has spoken with announcers around the world can be much less happy when rival stations have a fresh news angle because their reporters stayed in court.

Chapter 8

Human Relations and Ethics

Trust and respect

A senior court reporter received a telephone call from an anonymous contact. He sat patiently listening to the caller describe a case in some detail and make suggestions about the qualities of the parties involved in the legal fight. After some minutes, he asked the caller: 'And what's your interest in this?' 'I'm just an innocent bystander,' was the reply. The journalist paused, then shot back: 'I've been reporting courts for 20 years, and I haven't seen an innocent bystander yet.'

It might seem harsh to take a cynical view of information sources, but this journalist had a point. Everyone at the court has an interest or agenda. Reporters want stories, lawyers represent their clients, judges (we hope) make fair decisions that survive appeals. Callers or letter writers rarely tell you about a case for fun. They might be outraged at what they see as unfairness or sharp practice. An enemy may be in trouble, and the caller takes the chance to exact revenge. A public-spirited citizen may want to expose wrongdoing. It will not matter much if you find the case and hear the evidence for yourself, but a reasonable way of checking the veracity of a claim is to seek specific information. Ask for the location of the court, the name of the judge hearing the case or the charges being faced. Try to establish the name of lawyers involved. Aside from making the dispute easier to track down, it distracts the caller from lengthy analysis of the legal problem. The speculation cannot help – it's what you hear in court that counts.

Some of the most difficult calls are made by those who have long-running legal actions against large institutions. The callers might have a good case, but it's often impossible to work that out from a single conversation. Plaintiffs inexperienced in their dealings with the law can find unproven conspiracies easily. They may be right, but you are likely to have limited time to get to the heart of their complaint. Typically, you receive calls just as you are about to go to court. If it is a legitimate issue, you will need more detail to understand it. Often, I will ask for a one or two-page summary of the case, if possible with hearing dates, lawyers' names and file numbers. This makes it easier for reporters to make their own inquiries. Emphasise to callers that they do not need to be great writers – you just want the basics. Many can talk about their case for half an hour without prompting, and most are capable of delivering a summary. Remember, the journalist writes the story and takes responsibility for it. If you defame others, or affect court cases, those judging you will have little sympathy for your excuse that it was a good story, or attacked an elite body that deserved it. In any case, a good journalist will want to be accurate. You will need to examine specifics before publication.

I have talked about good behaviour in court in Chapter 2. Media law guides insist on the need for this, not least as an aspect of cultivating the human relations that will get you a good story. Above all, don't do anything to interrupt the judicial process. If you make jokes when the judge is summing up in a murder trial you are obviously destroying your chances. The long-term benefit for the reporter is gaining respect and therefore the trust necessary for ready access to information. Journalists working at the courts rely on contacts, in part because the bureaucracy has no particular interest in making sure they stay up to date.

Some newspapers help media status within the legal system by publishing court lists (usually higher court hearings) for free. The newspaper space would cost an ordinary advertiser tens, if not hundreds, of thousands of dollars each year. The newspaper gains an almost guaranteed group of readers from lawyers and others involved in the law as readers. They are a handy audience to sell to advertisers, but the process also helps the court reporter. At *The Age*, until recent years, the Supreme Court reporter received hard copies of the various lists and placed them in an envelope each night for a courier to collect. The lists would then be sent down to the newspaper for publication the next day. It was not a difficult task for the reporter, even though it had to be performed close to the deadline for the next day's paper. You might have been making calls, checking facts, or working on multiple stories, but you could not forget the court list. Phone calls from judges' associates or court officials the next day reminded you very quickly.

The payoff in pre-internet days was an earlier sighting of the court lists and a chance to speak with regular contacts. Associates and clerks rang semi-regularly to make late changes in the list, usually when the reporter was under even more deadline pressure. But successful changes were rewarded with compliments and perhaps a small measure of trust. Legal officers are critical of journalists. They react better when someone seen to be reliable asks a hard question or wants access to information. Years after contractors began collecting the court lists by email, the occasional late change still finds its way to the Supreme Court desk. I will always make the call to effect the change.

Courts and reporters have worked hard over the years to improve access to information, but daily calls still are made to police, court officials and lawyers in an effort to make sense of the dozens of courts and hundreds of cases within the system. One senior reporter referred to some old-fashioned officials as the 'keepers of secrets', who were smugly satisfied that they had the power to refuse queries. Others were more forthcoming, seeing themselves as pseudo-journalists, having axes to grind or wanting to be a silent part of getting information to the public. One night, a court contact left a writ lodged in a case involving footballers on the desks of two competing reporters at the courts. After checking with the club concerned, each of us wrote a story for the next day's papers. Apparently this upset a senior sport reporter at the other publication because he believed he had the story exclusively. Some of his colleagues reportedly blamed the other court reporter for telling me about the story, but they could not have been further from the truth. Each of us received the information independently, presumably because we had the respect of our source.

I cannot emphasise enough that respect and trust are essential for journalists operating within the legal system. Relatively few press releases are sent to inform or persuade about issues. Instead, court reporters check information daily and try to develop reputations for accuracy and fairness. One Magistrates Court reporter said she could call solicitors who trusted her to ask about scheduled hearings. 'When, in the morning, you've got five cases (to cover) and there's only one of you, you can ring (the lawyers) and say: "Is your client going to be pleading up today?" and over the phone they say: "It's going to be adjourned." I don't need to be in court for three hours to wait for it to be mentioned to get the (adjournment) date.'

The same reporter said prosecutors sometimes gave her an informal summary of a case, which let her decide whether to stay. During a hearing in a murder case, she took advantage of a break in proceedings to speak with the prosecutor. 'She told me what it was and it wasn't good enough (to stay and cover the case) because on that day we had other things (to report),' the journalist said. 'But the (wire service) reporter hadn't asked. He stayed in there all day. He wrote a story and, oddly enough, the (important details) didn't even come out at all.'

The danger is that reporters could be fooled because they rely too much on their contacts and not enough on their judgment at court. But each day they must make quick and occasionally wrong choices about which cases to report. Often, a number of interesting matters will be heard in different courts at the same time. Journalists cannot arrange to have one heard later for their convenience. They are at the mercy of the system. If they depend heavily on regular contacts, it is to refine the day's work to make sure they are where they should be and at the right time to hear the evidence they seek. These are some of the contacts and their relationships with court reporters.

Court staff

Each year, reporters at the Victorian Supreme Court enter one of the court-organised football tipping competitions. The current favourite is one in which an entire season's tips are entered at the start of the year. The results are tabled at the end of the year at a grand ceremony at a local bowls club. Journalists with offices at the court are invited to some staff farewells and the Christmas party, which is usually held near the pressroom. Most staff members keep their distance, but these are opportunities for informal chats with judges and senior court officials.

At least one innovation for information access was discussed over a plate of roast beef and salad and a glass of wine at a Christmas function. The important part of a relationship with court staff is for each to remember his or her role. No matter how friendly you are, each of you has a job to do. Journalists are not part of the court and should not see themselves that way. Sooner or later, they will write stories that displease bureaucrats or court officials. Some contacts will be upset. They will question the motives for the article, or ask 'Don't you know better than that?' But you and they should know it's not a reporter's job to keep the court's secrets.

Judicial officers vary greatly in the instructions they give their associates or clerks. Some refuse to let their staff speak with reporters, even informally, about a case due to be heard. Others, especially those who trust and come to know you, can be enlightening. The morning ring-around, practised by journalists throughout the country, can be frustrating, especially if all your competitors are making the same calls at roughly the same time. One television reporter said judges' associates or magistrates' clerks might be too busy, media haters, or unappreciative of what sorts of cases would constitute news stories. They will give you an impression of a story, but miss out the detail that actually makes it a crackerjack yarn. So one of the challenges in the morning is getting to something that might actually be worth reporting.

Usually, I make it clear in initial conversations with legal officers that I am not looking for comments or information to be used in a story. Be clear about the information you are seeking and be ready with a follow-up question if the response is short. One past contact was generally grumpy with everyone, but would pass on information, even if to deny a rumour, if asked the right question. It sounds very basic, but good manners and honesty about your purpose go a long way with contacts.

Victims and the public

Think of a common image from news reports of court stories. A group of reporters, camera operators, sound technicians and photographers wait outside a court building. Victims or their relatives are interviewed as they leave. 'How do you feel about the sentence? Tell us about your son,' they are asked. Family members read from hand-written speeches or struggle to suppress their emotions. They walk down the street, surrounded by the media posse as they are filmed and photographed. The images provide footage for the television news story; the interviews are played first on radio. Newspapers often will run the most dramatic photographs next to their reports.

The interviews can be confronting. Some relatives are happy to talk; some make arrangements with television current affairs programs. One in recent memory regularly telephoned reporters offering photographs and different angles on a family member who had been killed. Others want to avoid the process. It is no comfort to unwilling victims that reporters dislike chasing them down the street for the sake of pictures. Competition is the answer – no-one wants to be asked why their opposition has information they missed. As criminologist Paul Wilson once reported, it is the reason why two journalists with, say, 300 courts to choose from will both be in the same case.

One reporter described it this way: 'You always pick up the opposition papers every morning and you have a look through the court stories and that's the first thing you do . . . If there's a (television) crew outside the court, and you don't know what they're there for, you make sure you find out. If you're doing the same case, you do the same case. But you're not going to go out of your way to tell someone you're doing something else. It's very cat-and-mouse.' Describing the competition as cutthroat, a senior colleague said he preferred not to deal regularly with other journalists. 'It's better to hear their arses getting kicked in the morning than ours,' he added.

Television reporters use an informal roster when they try to contact potential interview subjects. They take turns in asking police, family representatives, and court network volunteers who assist victims and families attending court if an interview can be obtained. 'I reckon the secret is to be honest,' one reporter said, 'and to not try and really spin a line (but) to actually explain why you're there,' said one experienced radio and television reporter. 'You have to be happy with yourself when you go home, and if you aren't being honest, and if you really just try to say anything to get them to talk, then you just feel so bad that it's not worth it. But you see it happen. If people get the yarn, and you don't, you say, "Well, good luck to them," because that's not who I want to be and that's not where I want to be.'

Remember, when speaking to crime victims or participants in civil cases, that they have been through one of their strangest and most stressful experiences. Most of us have seen courts on the television, but few have been to the courtroom, let alone been part of the confrontational process. Win or lose, it's a vulnerable time for those involved. Imagine their feelings when they leave the hearing. Then they must negotiate questions by strangers who will stir up the emotions again. Even those who agree to speak are grateful when the interview is over.

Reporters' accounts of another case showed one way not to approach a court participant. According to the story, a number of journalists were waiting to speak with the father of an injured child. The child benefited from a negligence finding against a company, and the decision was handed down late in the day. Emotional and seemingly relieved, the father said he was not ready to talk when approached by the media. 'Some of us have got deadlines,' the reporter told him, showing no obvious sympathy, before racing off to file his story. The end of a legal fight that stretched over years, and his child's welfare, was more important to him. Luckily, he was happy to say a few words after others at the scene gave him some space.

At the opposite extreme was the ABC radio reporter mentioned on page 118. She showed great sensitivity in her interview with a dying man who said he had brought a successful damages claim to help provide for his family and warn others about the dangers of his industry. The reporter gently asked him about his illness and family and the message he wanted to send. He responded with moving comments. The irony, as I said earlier, was that the interview was aired once or twice only because its timing made it too late for the day's main bulletins.

Lawyers and public relations

Dealing with lawyers can be the best and worst experiences associated with court reporting. Their attitudes towards journalists range from friendship and openness to disdain bordering on hatred. Always remember that they are representing their clients. Most, whether barristers or solicitors, are happy to correct or confirm details from court proceedings for the sake of accuracy. Some are more inquisitive about the details of the story being written. Many will insist, even half-jokingly, that the reporter should 'make sure you put my name in, and spell it right'. A number of journalists rely on lunches or regular contact with their favourite barristers or solicitors as a device for finding stories. A friend of one lawyer occasionally leaves messages at our office when his mate has interesting or unusual cases before the courts.

Large law firms have more structured ways of contacting the media, with either in-house public relations officers or hired PR consultants previewing cases, delivering comment or organising press conferences. One television journalist complained that she started covering courts to get away from the public relations industry, but her job was changing. Nevertheless, most daily talk is with lawyers (and police prosecutors in the Magistrates Court) as cases take place.

Like others in the court system, lawyers are more helpful to those they trust. They are cautious of the media because they know judges dislike legal battles being fought outside the courtroom. Solicitors have been criticised for handing documents to journalists during trials, or making strong statements on the steps of the court. If you approach lawyers after a hearing, wait until they have spoken with their clients or opponents at the bar table, and make it clear what you want from them. The easiest response by a reluctant solicitor is that he or she does not comment to the media. Mostly, a court reporter will not need comment, but you might want to clarify the meaning of a submission, check names and dates, ask for access to a document or ask about witnesses to be called later in a hearing. None of these requests require public statements. If lawyers realise this, they are more likely to be helpful, especially if they see that reporters are making an effort to be accurate.

The exceptions can be solicitors employed by government. As discussed in our reality reporting exercise in Chapter 9, one said he could not confirm basic details like a barrister's first name because his contract forbade him to speak with journalists at all.

Eventually the barrister helped reporters obtain that state secret, but little else. Governments should not be surprised if media representatives spend more time with plaintiffs' lawyers in controversial cases because they have an interest in telling the public about the case.

Journalists should be cautious when lawyers are willing to talk at length but insist that the entire conversation is off the record. This is a protective device, to plant an idea or information in the reporter's mind without taking responsibility for it. Sometimes it does not matter. If you received a call giving details of an upcoming court case, it might be necessary only to know where and when it will start, so you could hear the submissions. An in-depth background briefing might be useful, even if it could not be attributed to anyone. The journalist should behave like a sceptical newspaper reader in that situation – how much of this do I believe if no-one wants to put their name to it? Remember the solicitor mentioned earlier who ended a telephone call abruptly after I would not agree to a conversation that was totally off the record? Often, as was the case here, a little more information can be obtained from a more helpful source.

Be clear about the information you want. Think about the best source for it. Be patient, but insist on getting it right. Police officers have tried to help resolve reporters' queries by estimating ages of an accused or victim, or trying to sort out a spelling without referring back to documents. Rightly or wrongly, you will be judged on the little details in your stories. Contacts and readers might ask why they should believe what you say about the big issues when you cannot spell someone's name correctly. Journalists frequently approach prosecutors, court officials, court media officers or the Director of Public Prosecutions because they have access to official information. Defence barristers sometimes say they don't have information about basic information like dates of birth or addresses, or state that they don't have instructions to give that information to the media.

Clever lawyers take a different approach. Rather than complain that media coverage of courts appears to favour the prosecution side, they build bridges by confirming the basics and speaking directly with reporters. One experienced barrister saved a criminal court hours of legal argument by brokering a deal about a suppression order during pre-sentence submissions in a murder case. Journalists wanted to publish details from the submissions that the lawyers believed would endanger their client in jail. The judge left the court, and the man's solicitor simplified the desired suppression order. The reporters would not agree to drop their objection.

'What would you like to do?' asked the barrister, explaining the problems the defendant would have if his name was published. He walked away for a minute, then offered a deal: no publication of the man's name, and the lawyers would drop their application to have the whole proceeding suppressed. The reporters agreed. The defendant appeared to have a fair argument that he could face trouble in jail if his name was published. Faced with a reasonable prospect that the whole case would be suppressed, the journalists chose the lesser evil. This is not a usual practice and it is not for the inexperienced.

It sounds silly to have to encourage reporters to ask questions, but it is easy to forget the basics in an attempt to save face. Courts and legal procedures can be intimidating, especially for non-lawyers. It is tempting to make it seem as if you know all about the law, when a simple question might resolve doubts. Judges, lawyers and journalists have argued that only holders of law degrees should report on courts. The argument is that the greater technical knowledge held by a qualified lawyer will ensure the public is better informed. Qualified lawyers will have fewer uncertainties about legal precepts and will know where to find the answers. They will better appreciate the context in which judicial comments are made and be less likely to sensationalise.

As a non-lawyer, I have my doubts. The lack of professional qualifications in a particular field has not stopped lawyers and judges dealing with cases involving medical, engineering, architectural, financial or psychiatric issues, to name a few. A general law degree possibly would be helpful for journalists. Bear in mind that lawyers approached for information in particular cases might have written the textbooks and have practised for many years in an area of the law covered in a semester in a general degree. Experience in court is also valuable.

Legal knowledge is not the only requirement for court reporting. It is just as important to know how the system works and where to obtain information. Critics may prefer legal, not personal, issues to dominate court reports. In that way, the uninformed and emotive views of victims, relatives and media commentators could be replaced by reasoned arguments about the principles involved in a decision. Some commentators may go over the top, but it seems hard to understand how principles can be argued in the absence of practical reality. To paraphrase one judge, some critics ignore the blood when they talk about legal issues. Real people are killed and accused, real families are affected. If those who complain about judicial decisions are ignorant, perhaps it is time to explain the law better to everyone, not just those at law school.

It must be hard for those working in the legal system to see mistakes and misconceptions repeated in the media. Perhaps it requires more, not less, communication between the legally educated and the uneducated. Take time to correct mistakes, find the media operators who get it right, and use them as your contacts. The beat-up merchants and sensationalists will change if their information flow dries up. But critics might also benefit from self-examination. Do they have careers to maintain by selling themselves as the public voice for a particular view?

Even though law firms have embraced public relations, some lawyers lack knowledge about the practical side of preparing for media coverage. Lack of access to documents, poorly organised photo opportunities, bad advice about court hearings and movable times for press conferences are some of the frustrations reporters encounter. You cannot expect perfection – circumstances change arrangements – but dealing with the media requires planning.

Organisers would hope to avoid the example of one law firm which persuaded print and broadcast crews to stand outside a registry as a personal injury case was lodged. Documents were filmed and lawyers spoke to the journalists, telling them that the plaintiff was at the court. 'Can we speak to him?' the journalists asked. 'I don't know, I'll have to ask,' a solicitor replied. Ten minutes later, she delivered the bad news. 'Sorry, he doesn't want to speak. Can we give you any more details?'

Public relations staff

The key to dealing with public relations operatives is to keep asking
questions. It might be helpful to have someone organising photo
opportunities and sending press releases, but reporters should not
assume they need only turn up. The PR operatives may have a
good relationship with particular journalists or media organisations because they have had good results with them in the past.
They might have a case that they perceive appeals to one outlet
over another. Asking for information means you should at least
get a reply. One media officer has a policy of answering journalists'
questions honestly and providing information, whatever professional relationship has been developed with individuals. But the
policy would include not advertising the fruits of a reporter's hard
work and research to others unless asked.

Always go beyond the press release. Usually, I explain my need
to see original documents to make independent decisions about
newsworthiness. If they are not forthcoming, go to other sources.
Also, make it clear the story will have less value if the release is the
only information available.

Ask to speak with a plaintiff in a personal injury claim, understanding that any comments made in the interview are not privileged and should be published with caution. Be slow to divulge the
direction of your story, but make sure PR representatives are given
a chance to reply on behalf of their clients. This would apply, for
example, when a court case finished, and each side made remarks
about the result, possible appeals, and their opponents' case.

One self-described consultant, after a proposed settlement was
announced, wanted to provide an off-the-record assessment of submissions made in court by the parties opposing his client. He said
his lawyers had advised him not to make on-the-record comments,
but he was happy to give the background of what the other side
really meant. He was told that his side's lawyers had many opportunities to make these points in open court and the court reporters
would happily turn up to hear them. Another PR officer suggested
her clients' opponents were wrong in claiming a case was settled
for a record amount because other larger figures had been paid in
confidential compromises. So when were these settlements and
how much were they? The officer could not say, because they were

confidential. She was trying to keep the term 'record' out of the story, possibly expecting that the word would help promote the article in the newspaper.

Attributing the claim of a record to the other side, and making a quick library check, we published the story, complete with an attributed reference to the claim that it was a record. It is always best to check such claims, even though record-keeping can be haphazard in the courts. The *Gazette of Law and Journalism* provides records for defamation payouts and contempt of court penalties in the various States. On one occasion, one law firm claimed a record damages payout, only for another firm to call the next day with records of higher damages awards in earlier, similar cases. A number of telephone conversations with the original firm resulted in a newspaper clarification.

Despite the difficulties, it is possible to have professional and rewarding dealings with public relations staff. Journalists' access to basic information at the courts has improved with the employment of courts media officers. Professional public relations officers, at the courts, law firms and companies, realise that journalists value independence. Those who use hard sell, or try to use their previous media connections to influence people, deserve less success.

Relations with other reporters

Working at the courts full-time can be a strange experience. Reporters get to know their competitors better than their colleagues back at the main office of their media organisation. They are obliged to share published judgments and sentencing remarks, will sit together each day at designated press benches and sometimes work together in opposing suppression orders. They might have one or two media rooms provided at the courts, where members of different media outlets congregate during breaks. Pool footage can be shot by one television station and newspaper from a court for distribution among other broadcasters or newspapers.

Legal and court representatives seem to see one multi-armed beast called 'The Media'. No matter who makes a mistake, each journalist is deemed responsible and our collective reputation suffers as a result. It is one reason why even unpopular reporters are set right if they make a mistake in a shared court pressroom. Judges'

names, technical points, the description of charges are the subjects of simple mistakes. Most conscientious reporters are happy to
be told, and happy to help. In my case, a dedicated and generous
country court reporter probably stopped me aborting the first trial
I covered, more than twenty years ago.

As a young journalist, I obviously neglected or ignored the ele-
mentary advice not to report about anything said at a trial in the
absence of a jury. As I jotted down notes from pre-trial submissions, the reporter whispered to the naïve city boy: 'You know not
to report that, don't you? It's *voir dire*, you can't use it.' 'Yes, OK,
thanks,' was about all the embarrassed junior could reply. After
that experience, it hasn't been hard to offer others assistance.

The tricky situation is when you or your organisation has a scoop.
Some reporters leave the office to file, others use mobile phones to
hide the exclusive information. Senior journalists from outside the
round might be used to chase a story. Experienced court reporters
will worry when a competitor has not been seen for a couple of
hours.

Searches of the courts are mounted, country lists checked. In
Victoria's County Court some years ago, two reporters received
independent tip-offs about a cult leader who was in trouble for
deceiving his former followers. Each discreetly made his way to the
court, only to find the competitor there. Never mind, a third court
regular hadn't arrived and wouldn't be told. About ten minutes
before the end of proceedings, the third man arrived. He listened
to a short piece of evidence, spoke to lawyers, and managed to
obtain a copy of the prosecutor's opening and some transcript.
Needless to say, he received a terrific run in his newspaper, much
better than those gained by his two diligent colleagues, who had sat
in court all day.

Back at the office

Find a story, check the information, write it and file it on time. All
this means nothing if court reporters don't communicate with the
editors and subeditors or producers putting together the media
product. The published story is delivered under the reporter's
name, but he or she is only part of the process. Editorial managers, from editors to chiefs of staff, contribute to the company's

interest in an issue and its placement in the bulletin or newspaper it publishes. Producers and subeditors, working under deadline pressure, fit the court story into the available time or space. The satisfaction of having a story published with few or no changes takes more than writing ability and knowledge of the case. Court reporters need to keep their colleagues informed and be available when questions are asked about their stories.

Despite being professional communicators, journalists struggle when they speak with each other. Ego clashes, misunderstandings, changing circumstances in a restrictive daily (in radio, hourly) cycle contribute to errors and problems. Assume you are the only grown-up working for your organisation and try to help everyone else associated with your story. Check spellings, update the office with developments and help subeditors understand possible traps if they change parts of the story. And be calm. The court reporter wears the public blame if something goes wrong with a story because he or she is credited with writing it, but it is infinitely harder to get a message to those in production if you are having a screaming match with the night news editor five minutes before a deadline. For further hints, see Chapter 6.

The Age has morning and afternoon news conferences to discuss the content and look of the next day's newspaper. For court reporters based away from the office, that means telephone calls to the State news editor before 9.30 a.m., when most cases have not started and after the usual 1 p.m. court lunch break. Afternoon court sittings make it virtually impossible to pass on messages before afternoon conference finishes. A quick telephone call to one of the evening editorial staff updates an important story and copy filed early makes everyone happy. Theories exist about the briefing news editors should receive in the morning, when reporters might know about a number of story possibilities, but have few definite items. Photographers or court artists are contacted if the 'definites' are significant enough, but what of the possibilities?

Some reporters like to tell the chief of staff or news editor everything they have, to let them decide what should be covered. It could be a reasonable strategy at outlets like the ABC or *The Australian*, where editors might understand how the story fits with others in a national coverage.

One former colleague disagrees strongly, describing the practice as effectively giving a manager often lacking court experience five headlines and asking them to pick which one they liked. 'And that's the worst because they say, "Oh, we like them all." What you've got to do, you've got to order your priorities. It's up to the reporter to say, "These are the best two stories, these are the ones that are going to get up. These are the ones that I'm covering." And if you miss a story, you miss a story. It's not the end of the world. These things happen. But . . . don't put everything on the chief of staff to say, "It's your call, therefore, if you make a mistake, my arse is covered." It's not about covering your arse, it's about writing the best story.'

Organising other (non-court) reporters to cover a case can be a challenging experience. Messages go missing, directions are misunderstood, and in one case a conscript refused to report on a sentencing in the Supreme Court because 'it was just an armed robbery'. It might be annoying, but it's wise to check that the fill-in is available, knows where the hearing is and is going to turn up. If you are seeking help because you have a number of stories to cover, give your helper the easiest one. It's likely that a cadet or junior journalist with little knowledge of courts will be sent to assist, and it would be inconsiderate to subject them to a complex hearing they would have virtually no prospect of understanding, let alone writing about.

At the other extreme are senior reporters who decide they would like to report on a court case but do not bother to tell the roundsperson. It is etiquette for a reporter who writes a story in an area normally covered by a workmate to let the roundsperson know. Most observe the courtesy. Those who do not sometimes compound the insult by dropping the story once the interesting early hearings have finished, leaving the court reporter to get adjournment dates and check on the progress of the case. Once that is done, the all-conquering hero 'surfs' in at the end for the result and the important page 1 or page 3 lead in the paper. Mercifully, this is rare. Senior reporters have written some of the best court stories by sticking at them throughout the legal process.

Another misconception concerns the availability of court files. Staff members unused to the closing times of registries seem to assume the court reporter can saunter over to collect files at any time of day – though to be fair, anonymous tips about writs always appear to surface about ten minutes before the registry closes. In Victoria, for example, files can be searched after office hours, but only at the cost of hundreds of dollars. In other words, the story has to be worth it. It is important to grant independence to others in your office by educating them about the registry office. Tell them the opening hours, explain the procedures and costs of searching files, let them go through the experience. Later calls for help are often made in a more contrite fashion.

Court stories breaking in the afternoon can be a problem for daily newspapers. News conferences have been held and photographers and artists are working on other projects. Earlier briefings to the chief of staff or news editor might have been short on detail about the late case. One reporter, who specialises in quirky, off-beat cases, said he would sell a late story hard to night shift editorial staff, but only if he believed it provided real interest. Editors were notoriously cynical about 'great' stories that emerged without warning, and photographers hard to enthuse unless they were given scope to produce a picture that was out of the ordinary.

'Nag, nag and nag the night (news) desk,' he said. 'There's no substitute for enthusiasm, but you must have the words "unusual, bizarre, funny or horrific yarn" to back it up. There are some journos who hold back (information about news stories) until just before afternoon conference, or even after it for dramatic effect. Sometimes if the yarn will hold (still be current if publication is delayed), you'll get a better run with a fresh (lead paragraph) or after getting a reaction.'

Newspaper subeditors begin work on the news story after the reporter sends it via computer. In theory, court reporters might have little or no input after writing the initial version, which then has to be fitted into a space in the newspaper. But the reporter's job has not finished. Perceived legal problems, unusual spellings, reminders to subeditors not to remove defence submissions from the court story can be outlined in messages at the top of the story. Subeditors have mixed feelings about these – some do not read notes left at the top of stories, others think they are invaluable – but they can be handy reminders. The reporter might have written a paragraph in a particular way to avoid offending a suppression order. If so, tell the subeditors – they are not mind readers. Make sure after-hours phone numbers are available to the switchboard operator or mentioned in the notes. Newspaper night staff have special curses for reporters who disappear at night, especially if they have written a controversial or complicated story. Copy the completed story and read it on the bus or train on the way home. If you see a mistake or a problem, telephone the subeditors. No-one likes mistakes, but they like them even less if they are published to thousands, instead of being admitted to one other person.

Source documents or notes from the story are also handy items to take home in the briefcase. A precise check of a ruling made in a court judgment is much more valuable than relying on memory. Conflicts can take place when those editing a story have trouble understanding it, believe the lead paragraph should be changed or want to use the article in conjunction with other copy and need to alter it. Calmness is desirable. No-one wants a shouting match when time is tight and decisions must be made quickly. If a subeditor or night news editor has problems with your story, get your notes or source documents, examine them, and argue your case if necessary. Sometimes others are right. It's easy to read and re-read a court story after writing it and find it makes perfect sense, only to have another reader spot a flaw. Egos should not matter if questions are asked. It's much more important to get it right.

Journalists working in managerial positions convince themselves that they are running the newsroom. They are wrong. Each newspaper has administrative staff who know where the pens are kept, can organise a last-minute air flight for an impatient reporter, and keep records of who is on holidays and how to get in touch with staff superstars who turn their mobile phones off.

These administrative staff also take the calls that court reporters miss from readers pointing out mistakes or giving garbled tips about the next case of the century. Skilled editorial assistants obtain specific details about upcoming cases and make our jobs easier. They must be praised as often as possible, as must staff librarians and switchboard operators. Court reporters probably use newspaper libraries more than most other staff members. It's wise to keep a scrapbook of your stories for easy retrieval, but librarians are invaluable for your work. Journalists should not need to be reminded to appreciate the favours they receive from other staff. Some do, and it's shameful to hear a colleague bark his name down the phone line, followed by a series of abrupt demands. The best at our craft should be able to speak with anyone from the Chief Justice to the cleaner and treat them with civility.

Ethical questions

The journalists' code of ethics has much to tell court reporters. Tell the truth, avoid conflicts of interest, do not let considerations like race, gender, nationality or sexual orientation colour your reports. Respect grief and privacy and work to achieve a fair correction of errors.

Privacy and its definition is likely to be the most difficult of these. The courts are a public place. They make decisions on behalf of the community. Media interests would assert that photographing or sketching participants in the legal system should be part of the open court principle. Members of the public, with very few exceptions, would see witnesses, the accused, victims and their families if they were able to attend court hearings. If media reports effectively represent the eyes and ears of the public, it makes sense that images as well as words are recorded.

Judging by some complaints, it is the method of getting material or footage that is the problem. Few are happy to see themselves photographed as they leave court. It is a hard enough place to be without someone chasing you down the street and sticking a camera in your face while someone else asks provocative questions. Often the subject has endured tough cross-examination, or heard a decision which brings home the reality of the legal process. Over the years many interviewees have said they felt no joy when a harsh sentence was imposed on a convicted killer. 'It won't bring my loved one back' is a common answer to questions asked about penalties fixed in homicide cases.

The other side to this is that journalism is a competitive business. No matter what the story, reporters will feel professional pride if they get an interview or angle no one else has found. They will also feel the wrath of their employer if they miss out on information that everyone else has. These are the reasons why journalists, photographers and television crews chase their targets down the street; they fear missing out more than they worry about the sensitivity of the situation. Negotiation has modified the effects of the media scrum. Police, other professionals and family leaders can act as go-betweens to make sure the media get what they want, while avoiding harassment. Smart public relations officers have performed a similar job. They know the value of publicity. Many understand the pain their interview subject will experience as they are asked to describe how they feel about an experience that has changed their life for the worse.

Good journalists will show sensitivity about children, and there are laws prohibiting publication of identity and image in many cases involving minors. But it is reasonable to argue that pictures of a child who has won a big personal injury payout adds much to the story. Unsympathetic lawyers and judges might say it adds to the emotion of the story media companies are trying to sell. The counter-argument is that courts are not only institutions that hear theoretical arguments. The public wants to know about courts because they are real. The hearings deal with real people. It is said that observers who visit courts regularly go for the theatre and drama, but it is the sense of reality behind court rituals and manners that is the attraction. If you watch the delivery of a jury verdict, you can feel the tension in the courtroom without knowing anything about the case. Whether it teaches or entertains, a court report can give the public more than gossip.

Industry and employer codes of ethics and conduct give journalists consistent clues about acceptable behaviour. In recent years, the journalists' union, the Media Entertainment and Arts Alliance, reviewed its code of ethics to check that its requirements were relevant. The Press Council and Australian Broadcasting Authority, and national broadcasters ABC and SBS, are among the bodies that produce guidelines for their employees. The following list of ethical considerations has been prepared using the guides as a template. In practice, reporters may fall short of the ideals expressed but ignoring them will lead to trouble, sooner or later.

- Be accurate. Pay attention to small details and check them. If court reports give any hints about society's greater truths, they will be ignored if media audiences find mistakes.

- Be balanced. Present both, or various, sides of the legal debate. Let the evidence and submissions tell the story, not your preconceived notions.
- Courts are public places, but personal privacy can exist. Respect the wishes of victims and their families if they say 'no' to interviews. If you need to film or photograph, give them some space.
- Honesty is important. Do not mislead interview subjects. Always return family photographs. In preference, use them at court, rather than taking them to your office. Be sensitive when asking questions. Never be flippant about other people's pain.
- Separate fact from opinion, or be clear when you are making a point. Do not misrepresent a situation or leave out relevant information to support your thesis.
- Think about your audience, particularly when reporting horrendous crimes. The public is entitled to know what is said in court, but some details can be upsetting, especially to victims' families.
- If you refer to details about someone involved in a court case, such as race, sex, nationality, disability or sexual orientation, make sure they are relevant to the story. It is easy for others to use prejudice to explain a crime or other social behaviour.
- Correct errors when they are demonstrated. Be sure that you are fixing a mistake, not smoothing over a complaint. When you are sure, do not be mean-minded in making the correction.

Chapter 9

An Atypical Friday at Court

Knowing about courts is one thing; applying the knowledge is another. In a textbook world, a reporter could choose the story of the day, turn up at the courtroom, scribble some notes, quickly organise an interview and photograph, and neatly compose an article which respectful subeditors would run in full on a prominent page of the newspaper. The reality is somewhat different. Conflicting timetables, judges who turn up late to deliver a sentence, the discovery that a competitor has been missing all morning, are typically nightmarish practicalities. So how do you convey that to readers? The following 'reality-reporting' exercise aims to give some clues. Current and former court reporters, from radio, television and newspapers, were given a hypothetical horrible Friday at the courts where potential stories exist in multiple jurisdictions in a crowded timetable. Using an hourly timeline, the reporters were invited to plot their day and choose the cases they believed were newsworthy for their medium and employer.

First, an apology to non-Victorians and rural dwellers. For practical reasons, I have chosen Melbourne courts and journalists who work or have worked in them. Some rules will be different in other States, and in other cities fewer reporters may spend their time at the courts. The exercise is designed to show the way decisions are made. I have not named the journalists or their organisations. Some participants were concerned that their comments in a hypothetical exercise might be taken as the policy of their outlet.

On this mythical Melbourne Friday, we will have representatives from a daily tabloid and broadsheet, television and radio reporters from the national broadcaster, a radio journalist from a commercial station, three commercial television journalists and a team from the wire service. Each participant saw the list of cases below, shuddered, then filled in the timeline. They were asked to include the phone calls they would have made to regular contacts and extra calls to get photographers, camera crews and others to the scene. Radio reporters were requested to give likely times for interviews with programs, as well as their news commitments. We will track the day, hour by hour, ending late at night, when many of the entrants are drinking from hypothetical bottles of wine after their stressful experience.

LIST OF MAIN CASES FOR AN ATYPICAL FRIDAY

MAGISTRATES COURT
- 10.30 a.m. (Melbourne Mags) Committal hearing for man accused of murdering his de facto partner's 10-month-old son.
- 10.30 a.m. (Dandenong) AFL footballer in court on drink-driving charge.
- 10.30 a.m. (Melbourne Mags) Woman charged with murder after stabbing her husband. First appearance in court. Could be 'battered woman' case.
- 10.00 a.m. (Melbourne Mags) Abalone poacher to face sentencing.

COUNTY COURT
- 9.30 a.m. Sentencing for culpable driver who hit and killed mother-and-daughter pedestrians as they walked near their home. Family members of victims have indicated they will talk to media.
- 10.00 a.m. Local sports coach accused of raping female players under his charge. Plea.
- 10.30 a.m. Priest sentenced for sex offences against schoolboy.

SUPREME COURT/COURT OF APPEAL
- 9.45–10.30 a.m. Four Court of Appeal judgments on appeals by convicted murderers. One of the four is an appeal against a life sentence imposed for the murder of two teenagers.

- Jury out in murder case. Jurors deliberating since Wednesday. Alleged killer said to have beaten his wife to death because he believed she was seeing another man.
- 10.30 a.m. Man being sentenced for the murder of his girlfriend. He stabbed her sixty-three times.

FEDERAL COURT

- 10.15 a.m. Two phone companies in fight over mobile phone advertisement.
- 10.30 a.m. Hearing of asylum seeker's challenge to incarceration at detention centre.

HIGH COURT

- From 9.30 a.m. (Floor 17, Commonwealth Courts building) Special leave applications. One case concerns two young women seeking special leave to appeal against murder convictions for supposed 'thrill kill' of widow, 70. Widow's family to attend court.

CORONERS COURT

- 10.00 a.m. Findings published on deaths of two children in speedboat accident. It appears the driver might have consumed alcohol and the children were not wearing life jackets.

8–9 a.m.

The **Supreme Court reporter for the *Daily Broadsheet*** is making an early start to work. She is walking from her inner-city home, anxious to get control over the busy court list in front of her. At 8 a.m., she and Melbourne's regular court reporters head to the office. The higher courts tend to start a little later, and the Supreme Court reporter will have a limited area to cover compared with some of her broadcast competitors.

The **Television One reporter** arrives at 8.15 a.m. She looks at the law list in the broadsheet newspaper and the Magistrates Court list online. A quick scan finds the court stories in the city's two daily newspapers. The more interesting yarns are cut and filed for following up later. Television One checks her personal diary and files for information about the upcoming cases. She sees the AFL player is appearing at Dandenong Magistrates Court, about 32 kilometres from the city centre, and marks it as a must to follow. The perceived audience of younger viewers favoured by her station is thought to be interested in the code, especially in a sport-loving town. Sportspeople are both celebrities and role models. A call to the police prosecutors reveals the footballer is likely to plead guilty. Television One calls the police officer bringing the charge and the local courts coordinator to seek more information. She plans to leave her office at 9 a.m. to reach the Dandenong court by 9.30. If she's lucky, her camera crew might film the player when he arrives for the 10.30 hearing. Before leaving, she makes a number of other calls. The targets include police media liaison officers, judges' associates, who are asked about the sentencing and pre-sentence hearings, and clerks at the city Magistrates Court, who are quizzed about the woman charged with murder.

Other reporters are arriving at their offices from about 8.30 a.m. The *Daily Tabloid* has a **pool of journalists who cover all but the County Court**. They begin checking court lists on the internet, ringing the various suburban courts and deciding who will go to Dandenong. Sport is big for their publication, and the AFL story is a must. They liaise with the County Court reporter and try to find out when the 'thrill kill' application is likely to be heard at the High Court. They check past stories for information about the Court of Appeal judgments. The perceived interest at the paper, aside from the footballer, is in grieving families outraged at low sentences (County Court case), allegedly evil men accused of killing babies (Magistrates committal hearing), sports coaches in trouble (County) and convicted killers who appeal (Court of Appeal and High Court). The assumptions change if the chief of staff requests coverage of one of the other cases, if someone famous is involved in an otherwise trivial matter, or if a long-running proceeding reaches flashpoint.

The **national broadcaster's radio and television reporters** call each other, as well as their contacts, to sort out their response. The television journalist wants to know where the best pictures are likely to be and how much file footage (images gathered previously and kept) exists for some of the cases. She will ask the chief of staff to send other reporters to Dandenong and the Coroner's Court. The latter assignment will depend on the presence of file footage in the vaults and parents of the dead children at the court for filming and/or interviews. The TV reporter intends to cover the culpable driving sentence and check on the sports coach plea hearing. The radio reporter also wants a colleague sent to Dandenong. One person might be sent to file for both television and radio. The radio journalist checks with the higher courts about their hearings. She will ask for another reporter to be sent to the committal hearing, arrange to pick up the appeal court judgments and Supreme Court sentence later in the day and attend the High Court. Later in the day, she will ask a court clerk for the adjournment date in the battered woman case. If no other journalist can be found for the inquest findings, she will let the story slide.

Scrambling is a regular pastime for the **commercial radio reporter**. He tries to cover all the courts on his own, which means he gathers a number of good stories which lead hourly news bulletins, and misses others. He will ask the **wire service reporters** which cases they are covering so that he is not in the same place as they are. The national broadcaster cannot run stories from other news agencies, but the commercial station is a subscriber. The reporter hopes someone else from his office can attend Dandenong. If the cases start on time, he plans to go to the culpable driving sentencing, then run to the sports coach hearing to hear the charges and coach's plea, and try to get the gist of the case for a short radio report. From there, he will race to the committal hearing, again wanting to record the appearance of the accused man.

At the **wire service office**, checks are made at all the courts, in diaries, and with police contacts. The reporters are concerned about covering the stories of the day, with special emphasis on those with national or international interest. The reports are sent to numerous outlets – local and country newspapers, radio and television stations, and to other news agencies around the world. Off-beat stories, crocodile attacks in northern Australia and items about big-name actors and sportspeople are easy to sell overseas.

Television Two says she will have checked lists and diaries the night before in anticipation of a freakishly busy day. Dandenong is definite – television news organisations love footballers in trouble. Assuming file vision exists of the aftermath of the pedestrian double killing, she will choose the culpable driving case or the AFL player, and leave the other of those two stories to a colleague. She has eliminated the sports coach, priest and murder committal as potential stories, and will try to pick up an adjournment date for the battered woman case later in the day. A spare colleague could be sent to the Coroner's Court, and the High Court case might be covered if her station had file pictures and knew the widow's family would be present. Aside from checking with police, and the city and suburban courts, she would also look at websites from a couple of large country newspapers, in an effort to keep in touch with some larger regional cases.

Television Three sorts out her priorities. The Magistrates, County and Coroners Courts are the focus of her day. The AFL footballer case is among those at the top of the list, but she decides to ask for another reporter to be sent to Dandenong. Her station has a great interest in football, and the memories of unsavoury incidents involving players are fresh, but she can cover the city courts more efficiently than a fill-in reporter could. She checks that the station has plenty of footage on the pedestrian deaths, but finds none on the boating accident. However, she also learns from legal representatives that the victims' family do not plan to attend the Coroners Court because they are too distressed.

The **Magistrates Court reporter from the** *Daily Broadsheet* has collected the court list on her way to the office. She checks her diary and the list, telephones police and suburban courts, and looks at tribunal and medical board hearing lists (some provided monthly to reporters). Another juggling exercise begins. She asks the Coroner's Court registrar to fax a copy of the speedboat finding and finds out from the police prosecutor about the progress of the footballer's drink-driving hearing. If it is a first appearance in court, or a guilty plea, another journalist will be sent with a photographer. No-one will go if it is a mention (short preliminary) hearing and an adjournment date will be gathered later. She books a photographer for the committal hearing, and has already arranged for a sketch artist to sit in that court. Fridays are awful days for *Daily Broadsheet* editorial staff. Deadlines are early, and it is difficult to get a story in the paper if it is gathered much after lunchtime.

No-one has chosen the abalone poacher sentencing.

9–10 a.m.

Despite a pooling arrangement (agreement to combine camera resources when trying to film an accused or witness) between **Television One and Two**, the footballer has arrived even earlier and given the media the slip. The Television One reporter is not happy, but she checks with police and court officials about the likely progress of the hearing. At a 'think-tank' with her chief of staff, **Television Three** has narrowed the story list to four: the AFL footballer, culpable driver, local sports coach and priest paedophile. Another journalist travels to Dandenong, while she concentrates on the County Court. She looks at previous stories and photographs to refresh her memory about the culpable driving case, and briefs her camera and sound crew. A court artist will sketch the three separate offenders. A third reporter has been assigned the sports coach hearing.

The *Daily Broadsheet*'s **Supreme Court reporter** has begun making arrangements. Associates at the Court of Appeal have agreed to keep aside copies of the judgments; Supreme Court associates will leave a copy of the sentencing remarks and telephone her when the jury comes back. Juries can sit for hours, days or weeks as they consider their verdicts. It is an unpredictable situation. The reporter rings her chief of staff to discuss her story choices and suggests a business reporter be sent to the phone companies' Federal Court row. She walks to the Commonwealth courts building, where the High Court special leave applications are being held on the 17th floor. After squeezing into the crowded courtroom, she listens to submissions and the result, and tries to talk to the widow's family afterwards. Already she has telephoned the newspaper's library for background information.

At the *Daily Tabloid*, the reporters complete their telephone calls, send an email containing anticipated stories to the news desk, and call the pictorial editor to ask for a photographer to attend the committal hearing. One journalist attends the culpable driver sentencing in the County Court, another goes to the Court of Appeal to pick up and reserve judgments, then heads to the Magistrates Court to check the lists and possibly attend the committal hearing. If the committal is ready to begin, a text message is sent back to the *Tabloid*'s Supreme Court office, where arrangements are made to collect the remaining appeal court judgments and cover the sports coach story in the County Court.

Television crews are gathering around the city court buildings. The Magistrates, County and Supreme Courts occupy three of the four corners at the intersections of Lonsdale and William Streets. The National Broadcaster's crew starts at the County Court. While trying to identify key targets for filming, the Broadcaster's television reporter communicates with her radio counterpart, hoping to rely on her for many of the higher court stories.

The **wire service** sends a reporter to Dandenong for the footballer, but the news desk must work out whether the only rostered photographer should also head east, or stay in the city office. The day's priorities are set: the culpable driving sentence, sports coach hearing, asylum seeker case and alleged child killer committal. The news agency has a Supreme Court reporter, who joins his colleagues from other media outlets in gathering judgments and sentences and in seeking a phone call when the jury comes back. The High Court application result will be gathered later by telephone, and attempts will be made to cajole the news editor into sending a separate reporter to the Federal Court for the asylum seeker matter. That makes four staff in total covering courts – unusual even in a sizeable bureau.

10–11 a.m.

Just before 10 a.m., the **Magistrates Court reporter for the *Daily Broadsheet*** asks court staff how soon the woman charged with murder is likely to appear after 10.30 a.m. She hopes to juggle her coverage of the woman's first court appearance with that of the committal hearing. She takes a sketch artist to the committal, where an opening address is taking place. If that stays interesting, the reporter will give the artist the name of the woman accused of murder and the court in which she is to appear. The journalist will leave the committal later, when an important witness finishes giving evidence, to make sure the photographer waiting outside identifies the right person. She will give the photographer a list identifying the witnesses, police and lawyers he has captured on film. The paper's **Supreme Court reporter** has headed to the asylum seeker case, and its **County Court scribe**, after reporting on the culpable driving case, and gaining interviews with the victims' family outside court, attends the sports coach plea.

One *Tabloid* **journalist** leaves the culpable case for the High Court 'thrill kill' special leave application. Another colleague is based at the committal, running down the stairs to the front of the court alongside her *Broadsheet* counterpart to identify photograph subjects. She mainly wants pictures of the accused, if on bail, and the baby's mother. The *Tabloid* team remains in constant contact by text messaging as its members sort out whether to stay at a case or switch courts.

Having completed interviews after the culpable driving sentence, the **National Broadcaster's television journalist** files a quick radio report, then heads back inside the County Court for the sports coach hearing, leaving her camera and sound crew outside the building. The **television reporters** at Dandenong have brought their crews inside the court to view possible targets for filming. They have no idea how long the hearing will take, or when it will be heard, as it is just one matter in a busy court schedule. If it were a final hearing of the charges, they, too, would be running outside the court when an interesting witness finished, to make sure the correct subject is filmed. Around mid-morning, they will ring producers or news editors to give more details about the story and pictures they have gathered. On this occasion, the police prosecutor outlines the case against the player, so the timing of phone calls becomes important. The prosecutor can be asked at the lunch break if a reporter misses something important. It is a riskier path to ask other reporters – there's no defence if you repeat their mistakes.

Television Three completes her interviews with relatives of the mother and daughter killed by the culpable driver. She attends the priest sentencing, which becomes a stronger story when the judge makes harsh comments about the offender's conduct. The sentence takes about half an hour.

After the culpable driving sentence, a **wire service reporter** walks across William Street to the Magistrates Court for the murder committal. He takes notes at the committal, and during a quiet period in the hearing writes five or ten paragraphs about the culpable case. He leaves court to file the story by telephone, and promises to write an expanded newspaper-style version later in the day, complete with family interviews. It is called a nightlead. The **higher courts colleague** stays at the sports coach story, but other County and Magistrates Court stories will be ignored, unless an accused or someone connected with the case has a national profile.

11 a.m.–noon
Competing radio reporters at court can see a lot of each other and file stories at the same time. Employers are unforgiving if a journalist has missed an hourly bulletin, especially if their broadcast rival has run the story first and has placed it in a prominent position. The reporters will listen for an important point or theme in the hearing, then write their stories as the case proceeds. They tend to leave court at about twenty minutes to the hour to file, hoping not to miss too much while meeting their deadlines. Today, the radio competitors at the National and Commercial broadcasters have different aims. The National reporter sends a story on the priest sex case, then calls 'programs' for a question and answer session. The 'programs' title refers to the shows broadcast by announcers at the talk radio stations. Announcers like to show the immediacy of radio by interrupting the scheduled items with interviews concerning news stories on the day they occur. In a case of national importance, the **National Broadcaster** could spend all day being interviewed by announcers from different States and Territories. Today, the interview will be local and short, followed by updated stories on the priest sex and culpable driving cases.

The **Commercial reporter** also has experience of interviews, and the need to remain detached from comments made by announcers. He sees his job as reporting, not taking sides, but will correct misinterpretation or add knowledge if necessary. He is still moving from court to court today, pausing long enough to get enough information for a short story, and checking on the progress of his targeted hearings. He will miss some details and cases, but he can provide regular and varied updates. One day he covered eight separate cases, competing against six reporters from his main opposition.

The *Daily Broadsheet* representative remains at the asylum seeker case. She has been committed to the hearing, and knows she has to stay to gather the complicated submissions. Lawyers appearing for any government are generally reluctant to speak with journalists; they do not want to be seen to be commenting on the government's behalf by answering questions. This is understandable, but it has extended on one occasion to a solicitor's refusal to divulge the first name of the barrister he was instructing. Mercifully, the barrister found a commonsense solution and showed his independence by spelling out the name. The *Broadsheet* reporter is wary of missing details in today's case and will not leave while it continues. One of the four **wire service** staff joins her in monitoring the asylum seeker hearing. He sends a story before lunch.

Away from the Federal Court, the scrambling continues. **Wire service reporters** file from the Dandenong case, the sports coach case and the murder committal. **Television Two** has sent another journalist to Dandenong, leaving the **court reporter** to cover the County Court cases then take her chances with the rest. She ventures to the High Court, intending to stay if the hearing and interviews are productive. Otherwise, she will check the murder committal or return to the County. At some stage she will ring her producer or chief of staff to discuss what stories she has, the length and angle she will take, and how many will be needed. On occasions, a reporter will prepare one longer item, in which she is featured speaking to camera, and a shorter piece read by the newsreader. **Television One** remains at Dandenong, having left her news desk with information about the other cases taking place. **Television Three** picks up the Coroners Court findings and checks on the Court of Appeal decisions. Her news desk is interested mainly in two stories – the AFL footballer and sports coach rapist. She will write a package (voice-over and interviews) about the culpable driving case. The incident footage and family interviews are very compelling. The priest sentence hearing turns into a reader voice-over. Checks are made with media lawyers about issues such as suppression orders.

Noon–1 p.m.

By this time, the **wire service reporters** are looking to send stories for lunchtime radio bulletins, particularly if a hearing finishes or a decision is made in court. The **National Broadcaster's radio reporter** has finished her second version of the priest sex story and her third version of the culpable driving sentence. A number of stories can be written from one event for radio. It means different information can be included in the short radio stories over the course of a day, and is useful for courts when defence submissions are made after those from the prosecutor or plaintiff's barrister. Complete balance between the competing interests might not be possible in each story, but it can be attempted over a number of bulletins. News editors also like stories to sound fresh and new with updated information.

Television reporting is a more selective process. The **National Broadcaster's TV journalist** has a full-length story on the culpable driving case and by now is telephoning her producer to discuss her choices. The production desk will want two or three court stories maximum, so big developments in the AFL player story will mean she is asked for a reader voice-over piece at best from one of the other cases. **Television Two** has found a story at the High Court and is heading back to the office. She saw no other television crews there, which give her a better chance of a good run in the bulletin. Television news executives love 'exclusives', which can mean anything from having the only reporter at a case to having the only television reporter there. First, she must remember to collect some of the judgments and published sentencing remarks from earlier in the day. If she is lucky, one might yield an RVO (reader voice-over).

Outside the County Court, **Television Three** records a piece to camera about the pedestrian deaths before returning to her office. She hears the AFL player's club will investigate the incident separately. The club's coach has given an on-camera interview.

As lunch approaches, so do extra tasks. The *Daily Broadsheet's* **Magistrates Court reporter** will ask the prosecutor at the lunch break about the witnesses expected for the afternoon's session and the following Monday, if the hearing is not finished in a day. That will help her decide whether to return when court resumes at 2.15 p.m. It will also help her to plan for the following week. Shortly after 1 p.m., she returns to her office a few hundred metres down the road, scoffs a quick lunch, and starts writing the baby murder story. She scans the Coroner's Court story and decides it will be worth a few paragraphs. A story of that length is commonly called a brief or short. After finding file pictures of the speedboat accident victims and telling the pictorial editor, she briefs the news-desk about the baby murder case (a 15-paragraph story) and the two shorts she will write about the battered wife and speedboat accident cases.

The **Commercial Radio reporter** has filed stories for each hourly bulletin since 10 a.m. and prepares to do the same for 1 p.m. He has picked up sentences and judgments in his travels, and uses previous stories he has written as background. On busy days like this, he will send a 'voicer', a report that will feature his recorded voice, for the latest story, and written copy without a voice report based on the previous hour's 'voicer'. That way, the producers of the bulletin can mix and match versions of the required stories. He plans to base himself at the Supreme Court press room in case the jury comes back with a verdict. He will also ask for an adjournment date for the woman charged with killing her husband.

1–2 p.m.
On a busy day, lunch is a time for gathering and consolidating infor-mation. Reporters will check notes, help to get photographs and write stories. The **radio journalist from the National Broadcaster** is deskbound. She is writing more versions of her earlier stories and a brief report on the battered woman case. She is also collecting faxes sent from the main office. Police and other prosecutors, law firms and the corporate watchdogs often send fax messages about upcoming cases or decisions in hearings already run. Even when it's hectic, the faxes are sent to the court office.

The *Daily Tabloid* and *Daily Broadsheet* keep gathering judg-ments and sentences. The appeal court cases are more likely to be reported if an appeal is upheld. In each press room, **newspaper reporters** are eating at the desk as they churn out copy. They know they cannot be late on Friday. Early deadlines mean good stories will not be run if they are not sent by mid- to late afternoon.

The *Daily Broadsheet*'s **Supreme Court staffer** telephones the in-house library to find some background on the murder trial. She wants to be prepared if the jury returns. Both sets of reporters keep in touch with their chiefs of staff. **The *Broadsheet*'s County Court reporter** has two good stories and wants to be sure they will both make the paper. Unless it is a major story, the *Broadsheet* is less likely to run pre-sentence submissions, so she knows she will need to sell the idea. Like her Supreme Court colleague, she uses lunchtime to write. Of course, that takes place after she helps photographers outside court.

Other journalists are on picture duty. They gather outside the Dandenong court, the triangle of court buildings at Lonsdale and William Streets, and the Commonwealth Courts building up the road. **Television reporters** also gather judgments and sentencing remarks. The courts allow the media two hard copies of Court of Appeal judgments. That means cooperation between competitors as they try to share and/or make extra copies. Whoever boasted about paperless courts did not include the media in the equation. **Television Three** starts writing stories for the 4.30 p.m. and 6 p.m. bulletins, then briefs an editor about the pictures gathered for the items. She makes further phone calls about other cases such as the High Court application.

The **wire service reporters** have all filed stories. At the **Supreme Court, the staff member** joins other journalists in examining the published decisions and evaluating them. He might need to file only one report on the sports coach case, and tries to assess his best course in covering the others. If the sports coach plea has finished, he will face an afternoon in the media office, which he shares with the National Broadcaster and *Daily Broadsheet*. The *Tabloid* has its own office in another room. As they write, the reporters wait for the jury. Most judges will not take a verdict at the court lunch period, between 1 and 2.15 p.m. If the jury does not return today, it will sit tomorrow, then most likely be given a break on Sunday if deliberations are continuing. Many juries will return verdicts in days, even hours. Senior reporters remember waiting almost two weeks on a country trip, only for the jurors finally to declare that they could not reach a decision. Depending on the importance of the case, the court reporters could be called in for weekend jury watch, or be asked to prepare background information for those filling in.

2–3 p.m.

At the **Supreme Court press room**, another National Broadcaster radio story has been written and recorded. The journalist checks her computer for stories sent from Dandenong and the committal hearing, prints them out and adds them to her files. Newspaper cuttings and saved stories are important for background information, particularly when you must cover cases in numerous jurisdictions. She finds a story from one of the appeal court judgments and writes words (no voice-over) for the newsreader to repeat. Her television colleague voices a piece to camera (she is filmed telling part of the story) outside the County Court before making plans to return to her office. The current thinking is to combine the sports coach and AFL stories in a package – one story containing two separate components.

The *Daily Broadsheet*'s **Supreme Court reporter** heads back to the asylum seeker case. She checks that her mobile phone is on a silent vibrating setting, which would let her receive a message about the jury verdict but save her from admonishment in the Federal Court. The **Magistrates and County Court reporters** return to their respective hearings. They will hope for early finishes, but will have copy prepared in advance if they are kept in court until after 4 p.m.

Work is continuing at the *Tabloid* **press room**, although one reporter is still stuck at Dandenong. She did not take a laptop computer – that would need to be organised beforehand from the main newspaper office. If the hearing takes all day, she will be forced to file her story by telephone. She will be writing it out on her notepad during any dull periods at the court. **Two *Tabloid* staff members** leave the press room to return to the committal and the end of the sports coach case. The remaining journalist is writing. A similar roster is taking place at the **wire service**. The **Supreme Court reporter** is camped in his office as he processes and writes stories. The **Magistrates Court reporter** returns to the committal, and colleagues are still at the asylum seeker and footballer hearings.

Television Two, having chosen the city court option, is back at the station. She is choosing graphics to accompany outstanding quotes on the screen, going through the filmed images obtained at court and finding an editor with whom she will construct the final story. **Television One** is making plans. She does her piece to camera shortly after the lunch break at Dandenong, and convinces her chief of staff to send a station truck, which carries equipment allowing her to file from location. The truck arrives just on 3 p.m. She sends back the footage already shot and her piece to camera. She then finishes writing her copy in court while listening for other developments. At **Television Three**, the editing process continues. The reporter checks wires and radio updates, to monitor what else is happening. She also rings police and other contacts to make sure no surprise arrests have been made. On this day, Murphy's Law dictates that another big story could break.

3–4 p.m.

The Dandenong case finishes at 3.30 p.m. and the footballer agrees to an interview outside court. The reporters and their crews wait in a pack to record the player's wisdom. He has pleaded guilty and speaks about the folly of drinking and driving. Unlike some sportspeople, who try to dodge the cameras, or walk past without commenting, he has attempted to throw himself on the mercy of the court of public opinion. He promises to speak to schoolchildren about the issue. His club has a sponsorship related to road safety, so this course is seen as prudent and has the backing of the player's manager and club officials. The **radio reporters** file quickly to meet the 4 p.m. bulletin, then write longer stories which are sent by phone for the 5 p.m. Given the traffic likely on the trip back to the city, they have chosen safe options.

The *Tabloid* **and** *Broadsheet* **representatives** telephone their chiefs-of-staff to work out the best responses. They also have stories pre-written, and decide to file by phone. **Television One** calls her producer to provide an update, then reads her story over the phone for subediting on the spot. She speaks to an editor about which images and quotes to use, then records her voice at the truck, which sends the material back to the station. By 4.15 p.m., all the footage has been sent and the editor has forty-five minutes to cut the story before the news bulletin. **Television Two**'s Dandenong reporter has an extra hour, and has left directly after the interview. He has sent information by telephone and communicated with his producer as well. His newsroom's outside broadcast facilities were not available for him, so he will be cutting it fine to have the story ready. Lawyers are on call to deal with any legal problems arising from the case.

The asylum seeker hearing continues. The case is set down for a couple of days' time, but the **wire service** and *Daily Broadsheet* **reporters** need to check some details. They wait for the 4.15 p.m. finish so they can quiz the lawyers from both sides. On her way back from Dandenong, the journalist from the *Tabloid* has arranged to pick up the Coroner's Court finding. She has finished her story but is checking her tape-recorder for any good quotes she might have missed. Her chief of staff has called and wants a smallish story on the finding, so her work will continue back at the Supreme Court office. The main reporter for **Television Three** updates her diary after her stories have been checked, timed and sent to Sydney for the national bulletin.

The reporters still at the committal hearing are pre-writing their stories as they wait for the day's proceedings to end. Photographers and camera operators are recording witnesses as they leave court. The County Court sports coach case has ended. He will be sentenced in a couple of weeks, and the journalists run to their rooms to meet their respective deadlines. Family members of victims have said they will speak at sentencing. It is a merciful result for the reporters, who are pleased to have the extra time for writing

4–6 p.m.
The **two radio reporters** continue to write versions of their stories. The Commercial Broadcaster has to be more selective – he has written six stories today, and keeps in touch with his chief of staff about which ones to rework. The National Broadcaster sends a voicer on the priest sex case, and a second version of a Court of Appeal finding. She telephones the High Court to check on the special leave application result and on the associate whose jury is out. The associate says just before 5 p.m. that the jurors have not returned a verdict and will be sent to a hotel overnight in

preparation for Saturday deliberations. The National Broadcaster is happy to tell others in the press room the progress report – they were ready to call the associate as well. Everyone starts making plans for the next day. The case will be left for other staff, so Sunday newspapers are called, as are managerial officers in wire service and broadcast newsrooms.

The *Tabloid* staff make a similar check and similar calls. The **Commercial Broadcaster** shares their room, and he begins to make arrangements. If he is lucky, he will not be called in, a handy result for his football team, which plays on Saturdays. The *Tabloid* reporters have three computers and share them to write their stories. They, and all the other court reporters, begin to check court lists for Monday as they are displayed on court websites from about 4.30 p.m. Diary checks are also made to make sure no country trips are scheduled. Employers like to encourage early morning trips to country courts to save on accommodation, but that means planning ahead so that a car is available early.

Television Two has finished writing, had her script subedited and has checked that the graphics for her story have been prepared. Her colleague made it back in time with the footballer story. She checks on the jury deliberations, as does **Television One**. They are rostered to work on the Saturday, so they will catch up at the court the next morning. The rostering result means they will have a day off during the week – not ideal for a court reporter. Television Two continues to help her editor finish the story. She will call the library if they need more file vision, and she writes copy for another story to be presented by the newsreader. Her rival at the **National Broadcaster** has been writing her story and helping with editing. She rings the lawyers to check on a legal point, and writes an RVO from the committal hearing. The High Court case was left for another reporter, and would have been covered only if successful.

The *Broadsheet* **higher courts reporter** writes her stories, leaving notes for subeditors about pictures and any potential legal traps or misunderstandings about facts. The *Sunday Broadsheet* has saved her weekend, just as the *Sunday Tabloid* has helped its daily court staff. The County and Magistrates reporters at the *Broadsheet* also prepare for Monday. They check diaries and speak with their boss about the likely prospects. This takes place after the stories have been sent.

Wire service staff have their heads down as they quickly process their copy. At this stage of the day, they are mainly filing for morning newspapers, but need to have the stories sent early, to let regional and city editors decide what they need. Sydney subeditors, who seem to have the knack of telephoning when a reporter has left the press room for five minutes, will call from time to time if they need more information or are unsure about a local reference. If the reporters have had to rush from court before they get their interviews to file, they try to persuade friendly colleagues (who read and sometimes use their stories as background) to let them hear the recorded quotes.

The **television reporters** have begun watching bulletins, starting with Television One. Those with stories still to run check with producers and/or lawyers to make sure there are no problems. They are checking diaries and planning for Monday, even those with the unfortunate weekend rosters. They look at the wire service copy, to see if there was anything they missed, or adjournment dates they can check next week. Television Three check the lists for local and regional cases, then writes Monday's court list for the chief of staff before watching the news on television.

6–8 p.m.

The **radio reporters** have left work. The National Broadcaster meets some girlfriends at the pub; the Commercial Broadcaster has headed to the football for a Friday night game. **Newspaper journalists** print out copies of their stories and take them home in case they are asked questions at night by subeditors. A quick perusal of copy while on the way home on the bus has saved more than one court story from problems. The *Tabloid* and *Broadsheet* journalists meet one of the **wire service reporters** for a quick drink in the city before going home. The court round is social, but tonight is not convenient. The **television reporters** make their way home as well. The *Broadsheet* **reporter** re-reads her story as she sits on the couch with a glass of wine. She has been filling in and is nervous. She wants no mistakes. Two of the *Tabloid* **reporters** receive subeditors' calls. One of them points out helpfully that the information sought was in paragraph five of the story. She watches the football at home.

8–9 p.m.

Halfway through the night, two underworld figures are murdered in the middle of Melbourne. Editorial staff work frantically to get the stories in the paper and on the late night television bulletins. The late-breaking news means some stories are squeezed out of the paper. The first victims? Go straight to the court copy. The lucky lottery winners who travelled to Dandenong thank heaven for Melbourne's AFL obsession, which protects their place in the news list.

Chapter 10

Suppression Orders

The right to publish is not absolute. Governments and courts assert free speech, but the right to attend and report in open courts must be balanced with other rights in deciding whether non-publication, or suppression, orders will be granted. Judges have made it clear that suppression is the exception, not the rule, a point that should be made to every judicial officer considering limits on publication. In 2003, Justice Geoffrey Nettle made comprehensive suppression orders in a damages claim brought against the then Governor-General, Dr Peter Hollingworth. A woman alleged that Dr Hollingworth raped her in the 1960s, when she was 19 or 20. She committed suicide after bringing the action, and the case was dismissed, her lawyers conceding it would be virtually impossible to prove the allegation.

Despite the orders, news leaked to Federal Parliament and the government was asked whether Dr Hollingworth had that year initiated legal proceedings for suppression orders. He had not – the suppression was requested on the woman's behalf – but Dr Hollingworth's lawyers asked the court to lift the suppression, and he defended himself in a recorded television appearance and two-page statement. The case involved a number of competing interests. The woman had the right to prosecute her claim, Dr Hollingworth had the right to defend it, and the public had a legitimate interest in knowing if the country's head of state was facing serious allegations. Justice Nettle said in making the order that the woman would reasonably be deterred from bringing the proceedings unless public disclosure of her identity were prevented. He also found that the media scrutiny of Dr Hollingworth and other defendants might prevent them from properly defending the action.

Justice Nettle said the open administration of justice served societal interests and was not an end in itself. He said the rules of openness could be modified if they destroyed the attainment of justice, for example by frightening off blackmail victims or informers, or endangering national security. Courts in various jurisdictions have the right to exclude information from being published in the interests of justice. The justification should be more than embarrassment, or financial loss, or the unsavoury nature of evidence.

The law has prevented identification of various categories of people. Alleged victims of sexual assault, children and those involved in Family Court and adoption cases have differing protections in Australia's States and Territories. Reporting of old, minor convictions can also be prohibited. I have already discussed the ban on identifying jurors. I repeat my thanks to the organisers of the Fairfax media law training manual for the following summary of restrictions in Australian courts.

Sex offences

New South Wales: You cannot identify the complainant unless
- the court gives permission
- the complainant is over 14 (or, if involved in Children's Court proceedings, over 16) and gives permission
- the story is published after the victim's death.

Victoria: You cannot identify the complainant unless
- No proceedings are pending regarding the alleged offence, and the complainant permits publication; and
- the court gives permission

Queensland: Unless the court gives permission, you cannot identify, nor can you publish the school or place of employment of
- the accused, unless they are committed for trial
- the complainant.

South Australia: (a) Without the consent of the (adult) complainant, or the judge, you cannot identify the complainant. (b) Without the consent of the accused, you cannot publish

- any evidence against the accused
- any report on the proceedings
- any evidence in related proceedings involving the accused
- anything identifying the accused.

This prohibition continues

- until the accused is committed for trial or sentence (in the case of someone charged with a major indictable offence, or a minor indictable offence for which they have elected to be tried by a superior court)
- until the accused pleads or is found guilty (in the case of someone charged with a minor indictable offence who has not elected to be tried by a superior court, or a summary offence)
- until the charge is dismissed or proceedings lapse.

If the accused is not convicted, approximately equal prominence needs to be given to this fact as was given to earlier parts of the trial.

Western Australia: You cannot identify the complainant (or their school) unless

- the court gives permission
- the complainant is over 18, not mentally impaired, and consents in writing.

Tasmania: You cannot identify the complainant or witness unless the court gives permission.

ACT: You cannot identify the complainant unless the complainant gives permission.

Northern Territory: Unless the court orders otherwise, you cannot publish the name, address, school or place of employment, or anything else identifying the complainant. Unless the court orders otherwise, or the accused is committed for trial or sentence, you cannot publish the name, address, school or place of employment, or anything else identifying the accused.

Children

Australian States and Territories restrict publication of material about children involved in court cases. The table below sets out some of the restrictions.

The media generally can enter Family Court proceedings but cannot publish accounts which identify any person associated with

Table 10.1 Restrictions on publication of material about children

	Definition of a child	Can you identify a child who is involved in court proceedings?	Are the media entitled to be in court?	Can you report proceedings (subject to rules regarding identifying the child)?
New South Wales	Under 18.	No, unless court consents, if child under 16, or child consents, if 16 or over.	Yes, unless court orders otherwise.	Yes, unless court orders otherwise.
Victoria	If charged with an offence, 10–17 at the time of the offence (but not older than 18 when brought before court).	No, unless court consents.	Yes, unless court orders otherwise.	Yes, unless court orders otherwise.
Queensland	In proceedings for offence – under 17. In proceedings for child welfare – under 18.	Not usually, unless court consents.	Children's Court – no, unless court orders otherwise. Not at all in child welfare proceedings.	No, unless court orders otherwise.
South Australia	Under 18	No, unless court orders otherwise; also need consent of the youth and their guardian.	Yes, if proceedings relate to an alleged offence, unless court orders otherwise.	No, unless court orders otherwise – also need consent of the youth and their guardian.
Western Australia	In proceedings other than for offence – under 18 at the time of the proceedings. In proceedings for offences – under 18 at time of committing the offence.	Children's Court: No, unless court consents. Certain other courts: Yes, unless court orders otherwise.	Yes, unless court orders otherwise.	Yes, unless court orders otherwise.
Tasmania	Over 10, but under 18 at the time of alleged offence.	No, unless court consents.	No, unless court orders otherwise.	Yes, unless court orders otherwise.
ACT	Under 18.	No, unless court consents.	Yes, unless court orders otherwise.	Yes, unless court orders otherwise.
Northern Territory	Under 18.	Family Matters Court: No, unless court orders otherwise. Yes, unless court orders otherwise.	Yes, unless court orders otherwise.	Yes, unless court orders otherwise.

the case. Reports can publish the outcome of a case, without going into detail. The exception, as mentioned earlier, is when the court releases names and publishes photographs on its website to help find missing children. The details normally suppressed include:
- name, title, pseudonym or alias
- address
- physical appearance
- job or profession
- the person's relationship with others already identified
- the person's recreational, religious or political beliefs and interests
- property interests
- a photograph or film footage of a person
- the identifiable voice of a person.

Some jurisdictions have laws restricting publication of minor offences from a person's past, on the ground that they have paid their debt to society and should not have less serious indiscretions mentioned in the public arena. The laws make it an offence to publish the convictions without consent of the previous offender.
- In New South Wales, the ban applies to most minor convictions of people, not companies, resulting in up to six months' imprisonment, excluding sexual offences. It comes into force after adult offenders have been free of convictions for ten years and children for three years.
- The ten-year period generally applies in Western Australia, but it varies according to the offence.
- Queensland has a ten-year period for adults and five years for a person dealt with as a child.
- In the Northern Territory, offences with up to six months' imprisonment are protected for adults after ten years, and for those tried in a juvenile court after five years. Sexual offences and those committed by a body corporate are excluded.
- Commonwealth laws have a ten-year period for adults and five for juveniles, with exemptions. Re-offenders are not covered.

Journalists will also encounter suppression orders made by judicial officers. The States and Territories have regimes allowing orders to be made, usually in the interests of the administration of justice. The restrictive system of the Family Court means that media interests do not brief lawyers to stand in court to oppose specific orders. The court's media office announces the missing child exemptions.

In other jurisdictions, reporters can either ask for adjournments to brief lawyers or send in lawyers to oppose suppression orders during or after the application. As a general rule, evidence or proceedings cannot be suppressed to prevent social embarrassment, damage to finances or reputation, or the publication of unsavoury evidence. South Australia, for example, allows suppression to prevent undue hardship, but applicants must show that the hardship is out of the ordinary.

Journalists will not necessarily receive notice that a party is going to ask for suppression, so it is important to get as much information as possible in court about the application. Knowledge of the issues will help you decide if you want to oppose a suppression order and will help the lawyers called to represent the media. Suppression cases can be a nightmare for media lawyers. They are usually called at short notice, they have no paperwork from the case, and they are not one of the parties. Court reporters can do their legal representatives a great favour by providing intelligence from the hearing. Listen for the information sought to be suppressed and the grounds for it. If counsel in the case want the court closed, and the judge or magistrate agrees, a telephone call needs to be made immediately. When a court is closed, journalists and other members of the public are excluded. Media lawyers are not popular when they edge their way into those hearings, but they at least have a chance of being heard.

Junior reporters should contact their supervisor – either a more senior court reporter or a chief of staff – if they are present during a suppression order application. Media organisations are budget-conscious and do not want to be calling lawyers to court unless they have to. In big cases, short-term alliances are formed between competing outlets to share costs and present a united opposition. Senior reporters are more often trusted to make decisions without consulting the news desk about suppression cases.

Major metropolitan newspapers have the resources to challenge suppression orders consistently, but this might not apply to their local and rural counterparts where income, budgets and staff numbers are smaller. A senior subeditor might be used as a de facto legal adviser, relying on his or her experience to avoid legal problems. In those circumstances, you might struggle to get help when defence counsel seek restrictions. If the story is good enough, and your media outlet has a connection to a larger entity (e.g. one of the bigger newspapers), it might be worth suggesting to your editor that the case be passed on. A smaller organisation could be lucky enough to benefit from the greater wealth of its larger sister publication.

The first rule of journalism is not to censor yourself. There are many rules which restrict publication, so decisions about publishing stories should be left to editors and media lawyers. Courts can be the exception, in the sense that some of the evidence is so graphic and brutal that mass market publications, concerned about the reactions of readers, will modify reports. The main television news bulletins are broadcast when children could be watching, and newspapers can be read at the breakfast table. Judgment among media companies varies considerably. Some will publish the most detailed evidence from murder sentences; others will pull back. At one trial some years ago, my newspaper decided not to publish details of the mutilation suffered by the victim of a notorious murder, but the decision changed when that evidence became crucial at a subsequent trial of the same accused.

It sounds trite, but the nature of some evidence gives new respect for the police and medical personnel who encounter it regularly on site, well before it is presented in the sanitised courtroom.

The parties who seek suppression orders can range from ordinary citizens whose lives are affected by court proceedings to government agencies and big business trying to protect commercial or state secrets. Listen carefully and be wary of dealing with business and government where suppression orders are concerned. They have the resources and inclination to ask for a whole case to be suppressed when prohibiting a name or a piece of evidence would do the job. If the media has a role in scrutinising courts, these are the people we should be looking at, to make sure our big institutions are not taking improper advantage.

On the other hand, we have to pick our cases. Despite the opinions of some judges and lawyers, the media money pit for taking legal action is not bottomless. Media executives and their accountants want to know they are getting a return for their expenditure. They will be more tolerant of in-principle arguments against secrecy in cases attracting high media interest. It can be possible to negotiate with the lawyers seeking the suppression in court, but it is not a task for the inexperienced.

I mentioned earlier the case in which a judge invited reporters and lawyers for an accused man to discuss their differing attitudes to an application for a suppression order. As we saw on that occasion, the competing media and legal interests were able to make an arrangement that allowed the hearing to be covered and the accused to be protected. In the circumstances, the media could have spent a lot of money for the same result. Critics would decry any negotiation from the open justice principle, but this was a rare occurrence that relied on the judgment of the players.

Court reporters can help themselves and the court by taking measures that aid the efficiency of the proceedings. Remember, suppression fights are often adjuncts to the main hearing before the court. In the Falconio case in the Northern Territory, suppression arguments took a week to resolve, delaying the committal hearing. In that case, the high local and overseas interest meant a lengthy battle was likely. But this is not the norm. Media interests can help their cause by taking a number of measures in hearings of lower profile:

- Find a suitable time for argument. It might not suit deadlines, but arguing suppression issues at the lunch break or after court can let the main hearing continue and at the same time show the court you appreciate the importance of the case.
- Argue for 'sunset' clauses if a suppression order is made. In other words, try to have an end point for the order, when publication will not affect the legal process. A name or evidence might be suppressed until the end of a trial, when control will pass from jurors to a judge. Requiring a further order to be made to lift the suppression can cause practical difficulties if the parties are not available or if a judge at the end of a long case does not want to deal with the issue.
- Narrow the issues. Find out what the applicant wants to suppress and sort out the minimum that needs to be done to achieve that aim, if it is legitimate. The assumption is that courts are

open and that orders prohibiting publication are exceptions. Lawyers and judicial officers can make many assumptions about the likely effect of publication on the administration of justice. They love the idea of ensuring that potential jurors are safe from prejudice.

- Media lawyers should be proactive, if a suppression decision is made, by preparing draft orders to cover the situation. The orders should be clear and simple – the worst are written in complex language which is capable of multiple interpretations. When queried, judicial officers are capable of denying the meaning was unclear, or worse, saying they are not required to give parties legal advice. The party requesting suppression is more than happy to make sure orders are vague and difficult to understand.
- Be slow to pick on small litigants. Find out what they want and see if there is a way around it. Judges are unsympathetic when a big media company is taking on an unrepresented party with limited knowledge of the law. Rightly, they want to ensure justice is done.
- When suppression fights are on, take the chance to remind the court the media has a role in informing the public. Media companies are commercial entities, but they give public protection by observing and reporting the legal process. Use the many precedents which act against secrecy. The courts have asserted the role of journalists as scrutinisers. Members of the public might be free to enter courts, but most do not have the time or inclination. Media counsel will have to pick their targets – some judicial officers have been stung by poor reporting and show little empathy.
- Suppression applications can signal a good story. Professionals will sometimes panic and ask for them to avoid embarrassment. A dull case can be enlivened by the details applicants are forced to reveal to support their bid for secrecy.
- Ask to see details if a lawyer or court official tells you that you cannot stay in court because the case is suppressed. Apart from statutory requirements, reporters should be able to stay in court even if a suppression order has been made. Those informing you can make mistakes. If nothing else, it will be helpful to know what the case is about and what has been prohibited.

Chapter 11

Future Directions and Issues

Attend a conference or seminar about the future of law and journalism, and it's a fair bet the talk will turn to televising courts. Cameras have been allowed in various Australian courts, mainly broadcasts of judgments and sentencing decisions, footage taken at the start of proceedings, and ceremonial occasions. Writing in 1995, Justice Michael Kirby speculated on the inevitability of cameras in court. He mentioned the Bobbit and O. J. Simpson cases from the United States and described the controls needed to stop the unacceptable distractions of wandering camera operators, whose presence might affect the testimony of witnesses. Almost ten years later, camera access is regular, though still tightly controlled. Australian television has no station which markets live broadcasts of the most spectacular murder trials.

Access has changed in other ways. Tape-recorders are relatively common and journalists have good opportunities in many jurisdictions to see, if not copy, a range of documents, statements and photographs before the court. A favourite trick is to use excerpts from videotaped interviews with suspects once they have been convicted. Viewers (or readers seeing still shots) find another way to get closer to the courtroom. They are not getting special treatment – jurors will have seen the film in open court possibly weeks earlier. Television may make gains through stealth if its operators are allowed to broadcast that footage soon after it is played in court. The obvious objection is that television stations will use the most provocative images that make the accused look guilty. The equally obvious reply is that juries are directed not to follow media reports. And if you cannot trust jurors to put the reports aside and concentrate on the evidence, what is the point of letting them deliver verdicts?

Increased security is another popular prediction. Controls have tightened since the September 11 attacks, but they were always a mixed bag. It was more difficult to enter the higher courts in Brisbane city twenty years ago than it was in other places shortly before the terror activity. The more disturbing trend is that of secrecy. Laws allowing secret courts, cases being heard in camera without being listed, and a tendency to close courts would be far more disturbing developments than the inconvenience of queuing for the metal detector check. Civil liberties groups and lawyers have protested, but it is about time opposition became more prevalent in newspapers. Politicians boast of having an open and free society, but secrecy breeds suspicion of corruption.

Speaking at a law for journalists conference in 2003, Lord Goldsmith said that court reporting gave practical effect to the legal principle that individuals were entitled to public hearings of criminal and civil proceedings involving them. He quoted the well-known legal writer Jeremy Bentham, who said: 'In the darkness of secrecy, sinister interest and evil shape have full swing . . . Publicity is the very soul of justice. It is the keenest spur to exertion and the surest of all guards against improbity. It keeps the judge himself while trying under trial.'

The Northern Territory prosecuting authority took a pragmatic path when it released a series of fact sheets and communications to the Australian and international media outlets interested in the committal hearing of Bradley John Murdoch. Mr Murdoch was charged with murdering British tourist Peter Falconio near an outback highway, and depriving Mr Falconio's girlfriend Joanne Lees of her liberty. The fact sheets gave details about the case and the legal system, and another release announced Mr Murdoch's committal for trial. Further documents gave advice about practical details ranging from media seating in the court to office hire and the best spots outside the court for television broadcasts.

Press releases during court proceedings are not unusual, but in the Falconio case they were advisory notes to the media explaining court concepts and giving practical information about the proceedings. They answered many of the questions that media crews landing in an unfamiliar city might ask themselves as they set up for the court hearing. Experienced reporters might have found the update about the legal system a bit insulting, but the releases gave the message that the authorities were worried that Mr Murdoch might not receive a fair trial because of invasive publicity.

Such an approach might be suitable for important criminal trials in other courts. The hardest part about high-profile cases can be the inconvenience of competing for space or information with multiple competitors. Courts wanting a good media image will win more friends by handling the organisational details well than by a hundred jargon-filled releases about policy and mission statements.

The fact sheet below gives dates, names, charges and uncontroversial facts about the case which would otherwise fall to prosecutors to relay, probably many times. Anyone who has had to drag those facts from lawyers or police officers will understand how helpful such basic information can be. Police and lawyers probably would appreciate the assistance as well.

FACT SHEET:

Prosecution of Bradley John Murdoch

BACKGROUND DETAILS ON THE FALCONIO COMMITTAL HEARING

Defendant:	Bradley John Murdoch, 45 (DOB 6/10/58)
Magistrate:	Alasdair McGregor, Relieving Magistrate
Prosecutor:	The Director of Public Prosecutions, Rex Wild QC, assisted by Anthony Elliott, Senior Crown Prosecutor, Crown Prosecutor Anne Barnett and Josephine Down.
Defence:	Adelaide Barrister Grant Algie, assisted by Mark Twiggs and instructed by Ian Read of the Northern Territory Legal Aid Commission.

Charges:

1. That on 14 July 2001, at or near Barrow Creek, Bradley John Murdoch murdered Peter Marco Falconio (then aged 28 – DOB 20/9/1972);
2. That on 14 July 2001, Bradley John Murdoch deprived Joanne Rachael Lees, now 30, of her personal liberty;
3. That on 14 July 2001, Bradley John Murdoch unlawfully assaulted Joanne Rachael Lees in aggravating circumstances (in that she

suffered bodily harm, that she was a female and Murdoch was a male, and that she was threatened with a firearm).

The committal hearing:
The committal hearing (normally heard in the Magistrates Court) is expected to be held in Darwin's Supreme Court No 6, which is being fitted as the Territory's first electronic court.
   The hearing will run for three weeks from 17 May and continue from 10 to 20 August and 25 to 31 August, before Mr McGregor RM (Relieving Magistrate)
   More information on the order of witnesses will be made available closer to the hearing.

Useful information:
• Barrow Creek is about 250 kilometres south of Tennant Creek and 280 kilometres north of Alice Springs.
• Bradley John Murdoch was arrested in South Australia and extradited to the Northern Territory on 14 November on the current charges.
• The Director of Public Prosecutors, Rex Wild QC, says 600 witness statements were gathered during the police investigation.
• All statements have been scanned and transferred to computer systems so much of the evidence can be submitted electronically.
• Details about the number of witnesses likely to be called to give evidence will be made available shortly.

Media coverage:
For security reasons, and to facilitate media access, the Sheriff's office in the Department of Justice will be issuing media accreditation for the hearing. Please contact Media Liaison Officer Jane Munday on 08 8999 7799 or 0427 880 083 for more information (international callers 61-8-8999 7799 or 61-8-427 880 083).

April 2004

The internet and its effects on courts represent the present, not the future. Ackland (2005: 29) reports the concern of judges that jurors in criminal trials might access information about an accused person's previous convictions by finding news stories or court decisions on media and other websites. Court and legal sites contain archived judgments and sentencing remarks, some stretching back years. Overseas sites will also contain Australian material, particularly in notorious cases. Local judges are concerned to confine jurors' deliberations to the material they see and hear in court. According to Ackland, legal changes in Queensland and New South Wales have made it an offence for jurors to conduct their own investigations. Juries are given more comprehensive warnings about the reasons for keeping them away from the public store of legal information. Prosecutors are being asked to conduct internet searches for potentially prejudicial material and request the website owner remove them until a trial has been completed.

The difficulty for the legal system is that information systems will become easier to access, not more difficult. Ackland suggests password-controlled internet databases to make it easier for suppression orders to be announced and found by the media. Australian courts do not have to contend with sites like The Smoking Gun or Court TV in the United States, which offer either public access to court documents in controversial cases or detailed coverage and archived information about cases.

The answer may lie in education, not control. Judges vary in the instructions or information they give to juries, but observation and unscientific anecdotal evidence suggests they are now more likely to explain more simply the serious task of making court decisions. In almost every trial, jurors are counselled to treat their job as an intellectual exercise. They are told they are in a court of law, not a morals tribunal, and are urged to throw away their prejudices. News stories, court decisions and commentary about Australian cases are featured on a variety of local and international internet sites. A cooperative system of requesting news and other sites to temporarily drop reports perceived to be prejudicial might be supported by telling juries that is what has been done.

If they are mature enough to find accused people guilty of murder, a decision which could cost years, if not decades, of freedom, they should be able to hear that the law takes the notion of prejudice so seriously that it tries to remove damaging material from their gaze. The notion of not telling jurors you are doing something because they might be tempted to check sounds a bit like hiding the jelly beans from the 5-year-old because all he will do is eat them in one session.

Courts have been proactive in using the internet to let the public know about their processes. Aside from the general information featured on court websites, media outlets have published weblinks to published court decisions as an addition to the news report of the same case. It lets the public see the source material at the same time as open discussion takes place. Judges will not have to worry that they cannot comment on their decisions – readers can see them and the full context of judicial remarks uncensored by the space and time demands of the media. Some jurisdictions have been faster than others in using this device. It takes organisation. Sentencing remarks, for example, cannot be written in longhand but must be typed and ready to publish soon after being read out in court. Some judicial officers object because they have not been able to revise the remarks if they have made changes as they are reading them in court. It is easy for the publisher to make it clear that a decision has not been revised. It is a small price to pay for letting a sizeable part of a community have quick access to a public decision made on its behalf.

If anything, links to court decisions would put more pressure on the media participants. Talkback hosts can be reminded promptly if they quote selectively or inaccurately from a judgment. Reporters will show just how much they leave out, and the absence of quali-fying or modifying information in their stories.

If media websites increase in popularity, newspaper court reporters might find their 15-paragraph story is reduced to six, at least the first time the public sees it. Same-day internet reporting of non-exclusive stories (why would a newspaper reporter with a good story want to give competitors advance notice on the website?) might mean changes in case selection. It is a lot easier, if the web-site is a priority, to choose proceedings with a built-in result (i.e. sentencing remarks or a judgment rather than a complex civil or commercial case) which can be gathered and disseminated in an hour or so. The trick will be to convince news editors that the complicated trial is worth covering, even if resources are limited.

Court reporters have been asked to tell their stories in a number of different ways. The traditional emphasis on the essential details, as outlined earlier, remains. But photographs, sketches, graphs and tables have become part of the process. Instead of writing one report, the journalist is likely to construct two or three in a major case. Feature writers take up residence at big trials. Reporters are encouraged to use a narrative style to replace the traditional inverted pyramid. Some constants remain. Judges, lawyers and journalists are suspicious of each other's motives. The best court stories will occur on the days every other journalist has a good story. And the smallest mistakes will lead media audiences to doubt what they are reading, seeing and hearing.

Bibliography

Ackland, R. (2005), 'Court in the Net'. *The Walkley Magazine*. Sydney: Walkley Foundation, February/March, p. 29.

Arlidge, A., D. Eady & A. Smith (1999), *Contempt*. London: Sweet & Maxwell, pp. 1–74.

Armstrong, M., D. Lindsay & R. Watterson (1995), *Media Law in Australia*. Melbourne: Oxford University Press, pp. 9–54, 98–134.

Austin, R. (Justice) (2001), Judgment: *Australian Securities and Investments Commission v John David Rich and others*. Supreme Court of New South Wales, June, pp. 6–7.

Bartlett, P. (2002), 'A costly trip over the media hurdle.' *Age*, 23 May 2002.

Bongiorno, B. (Justice) (2002), Judgment: *Jelena Popovic v Herald and Weekly Times Limited and Andrew Bolt*. Supreme Court of Victoria, June, pp. 1–11.

Byrne, D. (Justice) (2002), Judgment: *Rolah Ann McCabe v British American Tobacco Australia Services Limited*. Supreme Court of Victoria, April, pp. 2–8.

Callender Smith, R. (1978), *Press Law*. London: Sweet & Maxwell, pp. 210–20.

Communications Law Centre (2004), *Media Law Training Manual*. Sydney: John Fairfax Publications Pty Ltd, pp. 1–72.

Conley, D. (1997), *The Daily Miracle: An introduction to journalism*. Melbourne: Oxford University Press, pp. 109–19, 245–60.

Connor, M. (2004), *Pig Bites Baby: Stories from Australia's first newspaper*. Sydney: Duffy & Snellgrove.

Doogue, J. (1982), *The Writer and the Law*. Melbourne: Deakin University, pp. 12–42.

Freeman, P. (1994), *Courting the Law: A practical course in media law for journalists*. The Metropolitan Daily Newspaper Publishers, pp. 11–31, 56–98.

Fricke, G. (1984), *Libels, Lampoons and Litigants*. Melbourne: Hutchinson Publishing Group Australia, pp. 1–15, 153–61, 175–85.

Goldsmith, P. (Lord) (2003), Full text of the Attorney-General's Keynote Address to the Law for Journalists Conference. Guardian Unlimited, <http://media.guardian.co.uk>, pp. 7–8.

Good, R. (1999), '*Erskine v Fairfax* settlement: Record verdict laid to rest.' *Gazette of Law and Journalism*, <www.lawpress.com.au>, pp. 1–2.

Gregory, P. (1994), 'Rape was not "very grave", say judges.' *Age*, 15 September.

——, (1998a) 'A bloody finale to dreams of luxury.' *Age*, 15 July.

——, (1998b), 'Journalist fined for contempt of court.' *Age*, 1 February, p. 6.

——, (1998c), 'Jury finds boyfriend guilty of killings.' *Age*, 15 July.

——, (2003), 'Magistrate's libel claim is upheld.' *Age*, <www.theage. com.au>.

——, (2004), 'Colleague murdered woman, court told.' *Age*, 6 March.

——, Suppression Orders Literature Review. Assignment, University of Queensland, 1999, pp. 1–15.

Handsley, E. (2004), *Trends and Issues in Reform of the Law of Contempt by Publication*. Centre for Media and Communications Law, University of Melbourne. <www.law.unimelb.edu.au>, pp. 1–19.

Harper, D. (Justice) (2000), *Ruling: Linter Group Ltd. (In Liquidation) and another v Price Waterhouse (A Firm) and others*. Supreme Court of Victoria, March, pp. 1–5.

Herman, J. (1999), 'The Courts and Media.' *Australian Press Council News*, <www.presscouncil.org.au>, pp. 1–6.

Innes, P. (2001), *Covering the Courts: A basic guide for journalists*. <www.supremecourt.vic.gov.au>, pp. 1–13.

Irvine, A. (Lord) (1999), 'Reporting The Courts: the media's rights and responsibilities.' Fourth RTE/UCD Lecture, University College Dublin, pp. 1–15.

Kaye, J. S. (Judge) (1998), 'The Third Branch and the Fourth Estate: A state judge pleads for balance in coverage of the courts.' *Media Studies Journal*, <www.mediastudies.org>, Winter, pp. 1–7.

Kellam, M. (Justice) (2004), Judgment: *R v Williams; In the matter of an application by The Age and others*. <www.austlii.edu.au>, pp. 1–10.

Kerr, J. (1998), 'Mud Sticks: *Erskine v John Fairfax Group Pty Ltd*.' *Gazette of Law and Journalism*, <www.lawpress.com.au>, pp. 1–8.

Kirby, M. (Justice) (1996), *The Globalisation of the Media and Judicial Independence*. Commonwealth Association for the Education of Journalism.

Law Reform Commission New South Wales (2003), *Report 100: Contempt by Publication*. <www.lawlink.nsw.gov.au>, pp. 1–14.

Lowe, N., & B. Sufrin (1996), *Borrie & Lowe: The law of contempt*. London: Butterworths, pp. 275–9.

Melbourne Court Reporters (2004a), 'Fun-Filled Friday at the Courts.' Responses to questionnaire for reality reporting exercise.

——, (2004b), Personal Interviews. February, March and October.

Naidoo, M. (1997), 'Newspaper and Columnist Guilty of Contempt During Quinn Trial.' *Age*, 23 December, p. 5.

Nettle, G. (Justice) (2003a), *Ruling: BK v ADB*. Supreme Court of Victoria, February, pp. 1–6.

——, (2003b), *Ruling: BK v ADB*. Supreme Court of Victoria, March, pp. 1–4.

New South Wales Court of Appeal (1998), Judgment: *Attorney General for the State of New South Wales v 2UE Sydney Pty Ltd and John Laws*. <www.austlii.edu.au>, March, pp. 1–25.

New South Wales Court of Criminal Appeal (2004), *Judgment: R v Tayyab Sheik*. <www.lawlink.nsw.gov.au>, pp. 1–30.

Nygh, P. E., & P. Butt (1998), *Butterworths Concise Legal Dictionary*. Sydney: Butterworths.

Pearson, M. (1997), *The Journalist's Guide to Media Law*. Sydney: Allen & Unwin, pp. 21–92, 121–66.

Robson, D., & B. Thompson (2004), *Newspaper Defamation Case Provides Analysis for Three Key Defences*. Findlaw Australia, <www.findlaw.com.au>, pp. 1–3.

Saddler, K., ed. (2002), *Fairfax Stylebook and Media Law Guide*. Sydney: John Fairfax Limited, pp. 300–53.

Sheehan, P. (2004a), 'The Contempt is Mutual, Your Honour.' <www.smh.com.au>, 8 March.

——, (2004b), 'Victims Sacrificed to God of Due Process.' <www.smh.com.au>, 14 June.

Short, G. (1987), *Laying Down the Law*. Melbourne: Thomas Nelson Australia, pp. 8–40, 70–140.

Spigelman, J. (Chief Justice) (2003), 'The Truth Can Cost Too Much: The principle of a fair trial.' Fourth Gerard Brennan lecture. Gold Coast, Bond University, pp. 1–27.

Supreme Court of South Australia (2004), Judgment: *Registrar v Nationwide News Limited, Registrar v The Age Company Ltd, Registrar v The Herald & Weekly Times Ltd*. <www.austlii.edu.au>, pp. 1–12.

Teague, B. (Justice) (1998–99), 'The Tension Between Judges & Journalists.' *Medialine magazine*, Summer, Issue 7, pp. 6–7.

Victorian Court of Appeal (2003), Judgment: *The Herald and Weekly Times Ltd & Andrew Bolt v Jelena Popovic*. <www.austlii.edu.au>, November, pp. 1–104.

Victorian Court of Appeal (2004), Judgment: *In the Matter of an Application by Chief Commissioner of Police (Vic.) for Leave to Appeal*. Supreme Court of Victoria, February, pp. 1–30.

Walker, S. (1989), *The Law of Journalism in Australia*. Sydney: Law Book Company Ltd, pp. 3–95, 135–215.

Index

For EU product safety concerns, contact us at Calle de José Abascal, 56–1°,
28003 Madrid, Spain or eugpsr@cambridge.org.

www.ingramcontent.com/pod-product-compliance
Ingram Content Group UK Ltd.
Pitfield, Milton Keynes, MK11 3LW, UK
UKHW012156180425
457623UK00018B/219